Additional Praise for *Exploring the Life and Calling*

"Gary Black Jr. has courageously pursued a thoroughly countercultural and crazy thing. He has written a book that unapologetically proclaims that the world needs professional ministers who not only have theological degrees, but who actually have the training and character to lead a community of people into a transformative encounter with the living God. In a world that increasingly views the professional minister as irrelevant or even silly, Black presents a renewed and stirring vision of theological education that is able to produce men and women who intimately know about life in the Kingdom of God. Our world is desperate for this."

Kent Carlson, Senior Pastor
Oak Hills Church, Folsom, CA

"In a time when the title 'pastor' elicits more prejudice than goodwill, many wonder why God would ask them to give their lives to vocational ministry. *Exploring The Life and Calling* serves as an encouraging primer for those who want to understand this calling. Gary's work offers a clear look at what it means to study the divine, but more importantly, he sets a practical course for those who long to experience the fullness of life in ministry."

Rachel Triska
Executive Director, Life in Deep Ellum

D1056743

new series from fortress press!

Foundations
for
Learning

How should students entering seminary prepare themselves for the challenges ahead?

Books in the series give students the vital skills, practices, and values, as well as a glimpse into the course content needed, for seminary and ministry school success.

Sign up to receive all five volumes and save 35% off each volume and all future volumes as they are published!

EXPLORING
THE LIFE AND CALLING

GARY BLACK JR.

EXPLORING THE LIFE AND CALLING

Cover design: Laurie Ingram
Book design: PerfecType, Nashville, TN

Library of Congress Cataloging-in-Publication Data is available
Print ISBN: 978-1-4514-8892-0
eBook ISBN: 978-1-4514-8963-7

The paper used in this publication meets the minimum requirements of American National Standard for Information Sciences — Permanence of Paper for Printed Library Materials, ANSI Z329.48-1984.

Manufactured in the U.S.A.

Contents

Abbreviations

This book cites the following versions of the Bible:

ESV   English Standard Version
NIV   New International Version
NLT   New Living Translation
NRSV New Revised Standard Version

PART

1

The Calling of a Professional Minister of the Gospel of Jesus Christ

I n my first lecture, in my first class, on my first day as a professor of theology in a Christian seminary, I took my stand behind the lectern, took a deep breath, and looked out at the eager, somewhat anxious, very devoted, and curious faces of my students, and made this simple statement: "I am of the firm opinion that as professional ministers of the gospel of Jesus Christ, those of you sitting in this room represent the most important profession in the world today. And therefore, that makes you, by association, some of the most important people in the world today."

Then I waited, earnestly trying to read each student's reaction. The non-verbal responses were many and varied. Some of the more cynically minded instantly laughed, thinking such a proclamation ridiculous, if not absurd. Others looked around quizzically at their fellow students, trying to gauge their own response based on the reaction of others. Still other students were quietly skeptical yet curious, perhaps even hopeful. Only a few smiled a knowing smile and slightly nodded their heads in agreement. What I soon learned from that first class lecture and have witnessed every year since then was that none of my students had ever heard of, or even considered, such a proposition.

Nevertheless, I believed that statement when I first made it, and I believe it is truer than ever today. For those of us who live and work in what is generally understood as Western culture, which is becoming an increasingly post-Christian society, the necessity for men and women who are well prepared to meet the steepening challenges of pluralism, relativism, individualism, and consumerism by proclaiming, teaching, manifesting, and leading themselves and others into the good news of life available in God's kingdom has become more crucial with each passing day.

The writers of the Scriptures well understand and laud the fact that the feet of those who bring good news are blessed (Isa. 52:7). Of course, this statement needs some further justification. It's not an attempt to inappropriately elevate the clergy to a preferred status, although I would argue that the profession of ministry could certainly use some much-needed rehabilitation in contemporary culture. The ministerial profession has fallen on hard times, for sure. Few other professional fields that carry as much responsibility and are so crucial to our overall well-being as a society have fallen as far and as quickly from the lofty heights ministers once enjoyed. Some of our other vital professions have been able to maintain, if not increase, their social status. But from the perspective of history, few could argue that today the clergy stand anywhere near the same favorable position they enjoyed in decades or centuries past. Thus, before we discuss in greater detail what a professional minister must learn and why it is so crucial that certain levels of knowledge and skills be acquired, we must rearticulate why the profession of ministry is both a valorous and honored role in our society and in the world.

To do that best, we can look at a statement from Nathan O. Hatch, currently the president of Wake Forest University and a leading scholar in the history of religion in the United States. He argues that throughout U.S. history, those professional fields that are "taken most seriously and regarded as most honorable are those with some evident connection to matters of ultimate concern." He also states that respected professions and professionals are those who "deal with what the culture considers important and dignified subjects."[1] To apply Hatch's reflection, with what matters does the ministerial profession concern itself? Topics such as the meaning and the purpose of human life, the existence and nature of God and all God's creation (the whole world), death, eternity, good and evil, love, truth, grace, community, and overall flourishing—just to name a few. If we consider this short list, perhaps we can see why, for nearly a millennium and especially during the period of the Middle Ages, the clergy was widely recognized as *the* profession that rightly deserved the highest of honor and respect. The simple fact of that recognition highlights the undeniable importance of those "ultimate concerns" that the ministry is responsible to engage in, provide direction concerning, and further our knowledge about. These reasons alone justify not only why the ministerial profession is worthy of social, cultural, and political recognition, but also why those charged and called to the ministry must be of the utmost character and quality, with a certifiable level of expertise in these matters. This is what it means to "master the divine" and why the classical ministerial degree is called a master of divinity.

Therefore, mastering the divine means being qualified to proclaim, teach, and manifest the Christian religion's understandings of God's will and way to humanity at large. This goal is achieved in many and various ways, such as administering the sacraments, instruction of biblical and historical Christian doctrines, Bible teaching, preaching, and sacrificial service to the various needs of those in our communities, all of which expressly manifest, or shine a light on, God's love and grace. In these tasks, ministers are called upon to shepherd or steward those placed under their care in ways that the people can understand the goodness of God and experience it within each aspect of their everyday lives. In pursuing these two goals, ministers bear witness to and guide those who are pursuing their religious faith in order to equip themselves as disciples of Jesus. Ministers also are learning to place their lives and confidence in Jesus' ways, modeling the means through which we can both know and do what is good and right in our lives, and can, therefore, manifest and bear witness to the goodness and blessings of life in God's kingdom. This is commonly understood as evangelism—the professing of testimonial witness to others of the good life one has discovered and the blessings ("Blessed are those who . . ."; Matt. 5:3-11) within Christ's trustworthy message for meaning and purpose to human existence.

The power to know what is good and right and the power to do what is right are captured in the New Testament term *dikaiosune*. This important Greek term is often translated into the English word *righteousness*. Perhaps no better understanding or skill is more important to the profession of ministry. It is the great opportunity and obligation that ministers of the gospel of Jesus are able to both know and do the right thing in their lives, as they guide and instruct others in learning to know and do the right thing in their own contexts. As in no other professional arena in contemporary life, today the Christian minister often sits alone among his or her peers as one solely devoted to *dikaiosune*. Ethics and moral theory alone do not have the power to change the human heart, nor do legislation and regulation. Therefore, the clergy, now standing relatively alone in our culture, have the specific task and service of being beacons of the knowledge of good and evil required for righteousness and justice to be made manifest in our families, communities, and world. The objectives for our institutions of government, law, education, medicine, and the arts no longer include the promotion of love, grace, truth, patience, goodness, mercy, faithfulness, and self-control. If those called into professional ministry do not take up this calling, it will not happen. What ultimately results from a dearth of knowledge regarding the differences between good and evil is well represented throughout the Scriptures. A general collapse in our social structures is the result. None of us can afford to experience the plagues that follow a famine of truth like that described by the prophets of old (Amos 8:11-14).

I have no interest in elevating the profession of ministry onto a pedestal above the other key roles and responsibilities of faithful stewards in the laity, who are equal co-ministers in their vocations, neighborhoods, and families. Nor am I endeavoring to form a new brand of Christendom, forged by trained magistrates overseeing all social concerns. God forbid. Instead, Jesus' vision of life in the kingdom of God includes every member of the body of Christ and every human being as maintaining intrinsic value in God's sight. Further, the interdependency among our Christian leaders necessitates a mutual submission of one to another as an act of love and deference to demonstrate to the world where the leaders' allegiance ultimately lies (John 13:35; Phil. 2:3). None of us is independent, especially ministers. We are created to live and work in relationships governed by love. Yet it is the pastor and priest who maintain that leadership role directed toward holding out the invaluable information about the nature of God, the ways of the kingdom, and the intention toward goodness that must be present in every activity and priority within our communities, all while bearing testimony of the power of God's agape form of love to transform every aspect of human life and history.

When the American social experiment was first forged in the New England colonies, there also began an integral reshaping of the ministerial role. This was largely due to two factors. First, the birth of American democracy began to shift the social imagination toward an ever-increasing search for, and exploration of, individual freedom. This included freedom in civic, social, and religious matters as well. In the first amendment to the U.S. Constitution, the prohibition that Congress may not forge laws "respecting an establishment of religion, or prohibiting the free exercise thereof" has come to be called the "separation of church and state" clause.[2] Over time, many citizens began to accept the notion that the state should not or would not be involved in religious matters. This change eventually eroded the credibility and authority of the clergy or professional ministers, who previously were able and willing to offer their wisdom and experience to mitigate civic concerns.[3]

It is shocking to some to discover that the minister's influence, though significantly degraded, still held significant sway long into the mid-1980s.[4] Until then, many newspapers reprinted the sermons delivered by local ministers, not as paid advertisements for a church but as a service to the community. It wasn't so long ago that the information and knowledge delivered from American pulpits was considered essential, beneficial news—one could say good news—for the community at large.[5] Perhaps we can get a better sense of how much has changed in our culture over two and a half centuries, and how far afield and overtly specialized or marginalized the profession of ministry has become, simply by considering the kind of backlash that would occur today if a news organization tried to pull off such a "crazy" notion. But why have the minister and the profession of ministry become increasingly marginalized?

Before we can begin reestablishing the credibility and necessity of the ministerial role, we must first consider the subject of religion as a social, historically developing institutional reality within our secular and religious institutions of higher education. It is there where we can begin to reconsider the proposition of religion as maintaining a verifiable and valuable field of study that surrounds an essential body of knowledge required for human flourishing. Thus, religious knowledge is as important and fundamental as the knowledge in fields such as engineering, chemistry, or psychology and should be treated as such. Religious claims of truth can and should be engaged on their own unique terms so we can publicly determine which religious dogmas and doctrines from what branch of faith or religious preference carry viable understandings of our actual world, which include human nature and their relations.

However, to begin such an investigation into religious claims, we must recognize some key aspects of religious thought. First, most religions, including the Christian religion, argue for the necessity of placing faith (also known as confidence) in the existence and effects of what we could call an alternative, or "heavenly," realm or reality. This heavenly or spiritual realm is considered to carry traits and potentialities that are uniquely different from the natural, sense-perceptible world we experience daily. Second, religious thought argues for a certain level of relationality between the heavenly and earthly realities. Third, the spiritual realm can make claims on the earthly realm, including human beings, and vice versa. Religion itself is often a means, sometimes the primary or solitary means, of navigating this relationship between the spiritual and natural realms. Through applying or engaging specific religious rights and rituals (prayers, worship, sacrifices, offerings, services), often the religious person attempts to tap into the power and resources of the alternative spiritual realm in hopes of attaining a preferred outcome or effect.

The belief in an alternative source of power and authority, together with the willingness to engage and relate to this reality, form the basis of most religious doctrines and dogmas. Sometimes religions can become sophisticated enough to form an entire worldview. Many religions tend to limit themselves only when a universally sustaining vision and purpose for all life and human existence is accomplished. History has shown it does not take long for a popular religious worldview to gain momentum and capture the hearts and minds of a population. A community that shares the same religious values is often stalwart in protecting those beliefs when both the individual and corporate identity center on a religious underpinning. Often, such devotion creates a significant degree of security in defining both individual and communal purpose and destiny.

When taken to the extreme and bent to ill purposes, religion has facilitated some of the most evil and destructive tragedies in human history. However, when directed toward benevolent, righteous ends, with godly values such as those demonstrated in the life and teaching of Christ, religion can direct and inspire exceptional human flourishing that allows individuals and communities to thrive in the blessings of truth, wisdom, love, and grace.

Therefore, in these ways and many more, religious thought and life addresses the universal, existential, and practical realities of all human existence. As such, religion deserves a proper place in our institutions of higher learning, and it is a necessity for all professional ministers to develop equal parts competency and character in handling the key issues and ideas involved in religious life and thought.

This high view of religion and religious life is perhaps not popular within Western educational institutions today. Over the past few decades, several attempts have been made to greatly reduce or eliminate altogether the benefits of religious thought and life. This is witnessed in the ever-growing secularism in our society, as well as the steady popularity of sociopolitical ideologies connected to the works of Karl Marx, Sigmund Freud, and Friedrich Nietzsche. While offering some profound and beneficial insights, each of these thinkers in his own way sought to extinguish the "fantasy," "irrational," or "intoxicating" functions of religious life. Thankfully, in the majority of our world, religious life and thought remains dominant even in our more intellectually "advanced" societies. Perhaps the reasons for religion's steady popularity are connected to the growing enormity of human needs for which religious thought and practice seek to provide insight and wisdom. Admittedly, some disastrously heinous acts have been done in the name of religion and by those claiming religious authority. Authors and scholars, such as Richard Dawkins and the late Christopher Hitchens, are expertly able to highlight much of the harm that has occurred due to unrighteous religious fervor. However, as tragic as the abuses have been, human beings still seek answers for filling their spiritual void from religious life, which demonstrates yet another situation requiring professionally trained and accountable ministers of the gospel.

There is much more we could discuss in relation to the devaluation of religion in contemporary life. For instance, Dr. Tomas Rees, a biotechnologist who reviews the effects and differences in religious beliefs as applied in our cultures, has argued that nations with more religious affiliation have a lower quality of life than those less with a lower rate of religious affiliation.[6] He argues, "The least religious countries are more democratic, more peaceful, have less corruption, more telephones, do better at science, have less inequality and other problems, and are generally just less dysfunctional." What Rees and others like him do not engage is the underappreciated fact that religions are different, each espousing different worldviews, which often proceed from varying concepts of the nature of God and the purposes of human life. That such a seemingly elementary concept is missing from scholarly inquiry is but one symptom of the universally naive assumption in religious pluralism that all religions are basically the same, or equal, and all concepts of God or divine beings somewhat homogenous. Such claims pay disrespect to all religions and their claims. All religions are not the same; very few are remotely identical. This fact is easily discernible when one seriously compares any particular religion against another.

Much of the drain of credibility from the profession of ministry proceeds directly from the growing absence of understanding regarding the irrepressible role and function religion has played and continues to play in human life. Therefore, those engaged in higher education—teachers, students, and administrators—have attempted to recapture some appreciation of what Christian ministers serving the religion centered upon the gospel of Christ intend to convey and provide. Likewise, renewed appreciation is what this series of *Foundations for Learning*[1] books endeavors to explore and illuminate. Perhaps now we are better able to discuss what benefits the Christian religion offers and what ministers of the gospel are called to (ad)minister in and through their communities of faith.

 Titles in the Foundations for Learning Exploring . . . series are intended for first-year seminary students or those who are considering seminary and other kinds of professional ministry education. The books in the series share practical advice that will give students the vital skills, practices, and values needed to succeed in their preparation for ministry. The series bibliography includes:

- *Exploring the Life and Calling* by Gary Black Jr.
- *Exploring Church History* by Derek Cooper
- *Exploring Practices of Ministry* by Pamela and Michael Cooper-White
- *Exploring Theology* by Elaine A. Robinson

Better understanding the concepts behind the words *called* and *vocation* are crucial if we are to successfully rearticulate the value of the ministry profession. If you were to ask ten people to define the word *vocation*, you would likely receive several different definitions. One person might suggest that "vocation" is linked to only a few unique occupations that specialize in the trades, such as a plumber, mechanic, carpenter, or electrician. Another definition might suggest that the words *vocation, career*, and *job* are relatively synonymous. Still another definition could suggest that a true

---

1. QR code URL: http://store.fortresspress.com/store/productfamily/311/Foundations-for-Learning

calling is, shall we say, existential—something akin to the idea that we are all called to follow our dreams, heart, or passions in life. Perhaps each of these descriptions contains a kernel of truth. But alone they will leave us far afield from the biblical description of the kinds of mandates given to those who were called by God for some specific task or lifestyle.

When we look back into church history, it's interesting to note that during the time of Martin Luther, the term *vocation* was reserved for those devoting their lives to professional ministry. In Latin, the word *vocation* has, in its root form, a combination of several words: *vocatio* is a summons, *vocare* is the verb meaning "to call," and *vox* is translated into English as "voice." Often early ministers understood a divine calling to be hearing the voice of God in a summons that calls them into the ministry. During the Middle Ages, following this call often meant being set apart from the rest of society to serve God and the church in some specific way. One result of Luther's revolutionary reformation was to cast a new vision for what it means to be called by God. Luther helped us to recognize that a divine calling is not restricted to professional clergy in monasteries who live lives of seclusion, but also includes innumerable leaders in all the various sectors of societies and institutions who engage people in every walk of life. Luther realized that all Christ followers are called to be salt and light to the world, and he came to the point of advocating, "A cobbler, a smith, a peasant—each has the work and office of his trade, and yet they are all alike."[7] Since the Reformation, a person's calling has come to include Christlike service to all areas, disciplines, and institutions within our society, which includes but is not exclusive to the church.

So what is the specific vocation of a professional minister? The minister has a unique calling based on the foundation of service. In fact, the root word of *ministry* is the same as that used in the Latin word for "minus" or "less." The idea here is to reference a minister as one known to serve, which in worldly terms is considered the "lesser" person. But service from Christ's vantage point is reserved for the greatest in the kingdom of heaven. Therefore, the minister of Christ serves by educating, training, equipping, and encouraging those under the minister's span of care through applying thoughtful inquiry, modeling servant leadership, and taking care of souls. Our ministry, then, is our response to God's call on our lives; hence, each ministry is as unique as the person called, since the talents and skills allotted to each of us are distinctive as well. Therefore, the world is full of ministers.

Professional ministers are unique in that they primarily focus on leading or shepherding others within our congregations and parishes to discern where and how each member of the body of Christ can fulfill his or her own unique calling in service to the kingdom of God through whatever means, career, trade, or job the person employs. At their best, professional ministers have made it a priority to lead others into finding and accomplishing their full potential within their spheres of influence, which together promotes the well-being of all humanity. In some ways, we could assign the minister the title of Director of Calling Discernment and Achievement. Through prayerful, thoughtful reflection regarding the ways and means of God, the teachings of Jesus, and the purposes of the church, the professional minister works in his or her vocation to manifest in and through his or her ministries effective action that benefits all who come into contact with the love and grace incarnated through God's church. Scripture makes it clear that all followers of Jesus are called into his will and way. Yet professional ministers are shepherds of shepherds, leaders of leaders, and ministers to ministers.

The calling of ministers today resembles the call of Abraham:

> Now the LORD said to Abram, "Go from your country and your kindred and your father's house to the land that I will show you. And I will make of you a great nation, and I will bless you and make your name great, so that you will be a blessing. I will bless those who bless you, and him who dishonors you I will curse, and in you all the families of the earth shall be blessed." (Gen. 12:1-3 ESV)

In the call of Abraham, God's blessing was not for Abraham specifically. The blessing was to be shared, highlighted, emulated, and implemented in all the nations of the world. In Abraham's demonstration of his confidence in Yahweh's will and ways, other "nations" (*goy*, or people groups, in Hebrew) would be blessed—would thrive and flourish. This is the same concept Jesus explains in his Sermon on the Mount. His exhortation that we are to be the light of the "world" and the salt of the earth is a repetition of God's intent to demonstrate God's worthiness to "all the families" (Hebrew *mishpachah*, pronounced mish·paw·khaw, meaning tribes, families, clans, or people groups) on the earth through Abraham and his descendants (Gen. 12:3). The whole world—not just the Hebrews, not just Christians—is to thrive as a result of God's relational engagement with our lives. The Hebrew word for "nations" is the same word we see Jesus using (*ethnos* in Greek) in what we label the Great Commission in Matthew 28. There, just as Abraham was called and then sent out, Jesus calls and sends his students out into all the people groups of the world to teach his ways and immerse new students in the good news of the Father, Son, and Holy Spirit. And Jesus promises that when we do these things, leading by example, shining our light, he will be with us, just as Yahweh promised to be with Abraham in his endeavors.

This is the call, the summons from the voice of God that inspires leaders, witnesses, ambassadors, ministers, and servants of the Most High God. The call hasn't changed. It won't change. The good news is that according to John's vision in Revelation, the great call of God—which began with Abraham and has survived the great struggles of world wars, famines, plagues, genocide, religious persecution, political upheaval, intellectual darkness, social ossification, and the ultimate attempts of human beings to deify themselves—is destined to succeed (Rev. 5:9; 7:9). The question for the professional minister is, "How do we can find our own story in this larger calling in order to assist those near us—our neighbors, whom we love—in finding and then abiding in God's vocational purpose for their lives?"

In realizing that professional ministers hold knowledge of the unseen realm of God's power, the ways and will of life inside God's kingdom, and the means of discipleship to Christ through which we are able to live in the power of his resurrection (Phil. 3:10), we can begin to grasp how the Abrahamic destiny to bring blessing and flourishing to societies at large is still active in the call to ministry. In pursuing an answer to my previous question, perhaps we can lay a foundation upon which our future generations of ministers of the gospel must place their time, talents, and treasures if they desire to further the message and cause of Christ to future generations effectively and responsibly.

Let me attempt to recap as clearly as possible what we've discussed. What good does the professional minster, either ordained clergy or persons in the wide diversity of other Christian callings, have to offer? The answer to this question is directly tied to the unique knowledge and skills that ministers must both possess and profess. Ministers of the gospel of Jesus Christ represent the knowledge of God and ways of God's kingdom applied in the lives of the faithful. This knowledge Jesus provides should be properly considered a "light to the nations" (Luke 3:32 NLT; Isa. 49:6 ESV), even to the point where the collective Christian community becomes "like a city on a hilltop that cannot be hidden" (Matt. 5:14 NLT).

If we just think for a moment about the grandeur and immensity of such a task, we will come to the conclusion that the ministerial office far exceeds the overseeing of the specific religious rituals connected to hatching (baptism), matching (marriage), and dispatching (funerals) of churchgoers as they travel their paths through this life. As important and meaningful as these rituals are, the ministerial profession carries much more gravitas than such reductions would allow, and is needed now perhaps more than ever before. Still, our current cultural climate needs convincing of this fact. This is our task.

The following books in this *Exploring* series will provide insight and direction into the key components of the minister's duties and responsibilities, which require intense study, practice, and skill development most often provided by colleges and universities that offer formal ministerial degrees. The necessary fields of knowledge and skills—leadership, team building, delegation, awareness of one's ministerial context, Christian and/or church history, missiology, biblical studies and exegesis, Christian theology, and the more practical skills such as preaching, teaching, practice of our liturgies, observance of the sacraments, pastoral counseling, and organizational management—must be mastered and modeled so our churches and communities flourish. This is not a complete list, and there is certainly room for additions and arguments. However, this list is a good start to begin our discussion on what skills our ministers must provide to those they lead and serve in our communities.

But lest we think the minister is primarily outward focused, Jesus reminds us that each of his disciples is to focus his or her attention equally on the more personal responsibilities of the care of one's own soul. These responsibilities include individual spiritual formation, accountability, and discipleship that will develop the kind of modeling and testimonial representation of the effects of the gospel through one's own life and ministry. Together, each of these ministry skills, combined with the application of disciplines such as study, meditation, contemplation, conversation, solitude, fellowship, and many others, can and have forged lives and souls of countless ministers throughout the ages, who have accomplished mighty deeds in and through God's power and grace.

Perhaps the most crucial concept that will enable the minister to accomplish his or her call surrounds that last word in the previous sentence: *grace*. Grace is what life in the kingdom is all about. Yet I would argue that we have become so familiar with the concept of grace that it's actually becoming unfamiliar, losing its power and vitality for the Christian life. There are perhaps many causes for this. I want to suggest there is one primary reason that must concern us here. In our contemporary understandings of Christian life, the concept of grace has been reduced to, or equated only with, the act of forgiveness of sin. Dallas Willard has eloquently argued that grace is the divine ability to accomplish what we could not accomplish through human invention or effort alone.[8] It is true we cannot forgive ourselves for our sinfulness, and therefore it is also accurate to understand forgiveness as one demonstration of divine grace. But divine grace is much larger than just forgiveness. Grace is also integral to effective preaching, wise counsel, courageous leadership, and knowledgeable teaching. God's empowering grace is vital, working in and through us to accomplish more than we could hope for or imagine on our own (Ephesians 3). More important than anything else we will cover here is the need for ministers of the gospel of Jesus and the reign of God's kingdom to recognize, count on, elicit, and then apply

God's enabling grace to carry out their significant efforts in order to attain heights previously unimaginable to the human mind.

This dependency on the power of God's grace is evident in one of the most powerful (albeit dramatically portrayed) scenes in the controversial and somewhat odd movie *Noah* from director Darren Aronofsky.[9] That scene juxtaposes two understandings of God: "the Creator" (Noah's understanding, as played by Russell Crowe) and the understanding held by Noah's nemesis (the Canaanite king Tubal-cain, as played by Ray Winstone). The audience is presented with a clash between two understandings, two theologies, two worldviews if you will, that undergird two distinctly different responses to God. One view represents a life lived in light of the power of divine grace. The other relies on the power of human effort and ingenuity alone.

These distinctions are spelled out in fairly clear detail through some excellent theological monologues. The independent Tubal-cain argues, "The Creator doesn't care about what happens in the world. No one's heard from him since he marked Cain" (which, according to the scriptural account, appears true: the Bible does not record God speaking to humanity from the time of the rebellion of the first family until God's revelation to Noah). Therefore, Tubal-cain and his people, the descendants of Cain, have evolved into functional atheists. They acknowledge God's existence, yet their lives are godless or what we might call secular: "We are orphaned children in this world, cursed to struggle by the sweat of our brow. Damned if I don't do whatever it takes to do just that." Tubal-cain represents the legacy of his forefather, Cain, whose will was set on self-determining power, for he was not confident in and did not submit to God's desires and means of grace (Gen. 4:1-16).

In contrast, Noah's worldview is represented in the narrative of the creation, which he tells against the background of the cries of those suffering outside the ark. Noah gathers his family around the campfire and attempts to calm their fear by recounting "the first story my father told me, and the first story I told each of you." In calling to remembrance the creation of the world, Noah illustrates a vision of God's immense power, purpose, brilliance, sovereignty and grace, which evokes confidence—or faith—in the family members' troubled hearts.

Similar to Noah's trials, Paul also learned through experience that God's grace is sufficient in times of suffering and weakness (2 Cor. 12:9). We, too, can learn to live, move, and have our being (Acts 17:28) inside the grace God has provided for our lives. This is why 2 Peter encourages us to "grow in the grace and knowledge of our Lord and Savior Jesus Christ" (2 Pet. 3:18 ESV).

We know how to grow in knowledge, but how do we grow in grace? We grow in grace by applying it and watching its effects alter our world to the point where, like Paul and Noah, we wouldn't think of escaping God's guidance and support. Ministers need to come to the unshakable understanding that they are never alone and are not to work in their own power. Unlike Moses in the desert, who disobeyed God's command to speak to the rock but instead struck the rock to elicit the life-giving water for himself and his people, ministers must resist the temptation to supercede the power of God's sovereignty and grace in their service (Num. 20:8-12). Ministers have the opportunity to wield the power of God for God's purposes and glory. If we abide in Christ and his words, so that his logic and his ways settle into our hearts and minds, we can ask whatever we wish, and the power to accomplish these dreams will be manifested in our ministries (John 15:7). Taken seriously, such an opportunity is overwhelming to consider.

Learning to steward the power of God responsibly is a lesson every faithful biblical leader, including Noah, Abraham, Isaac, Jacob, Joseph, Elijah, David, Daniel, John the Baptist, Peter, Paul, and even Jesus himself, came to understand. The mighty hand, the mighty arm of God is God's grace. The minister of God comes to know this hand of guidance and its strength to overcome even the most ominous and troubling of obstacles. This has not changed and will not change. Obstacles build confidence. Without learning to overcome them through the power and provision of God we simply can't attain the potential available to experience a with-God type of existence (Heb. 11:6). Thanks be to God!

Questions for Exploration

1. Do you agree that professional ministers are some of the most important people in the world? Why or why not?

2. Have you ever considered religion as containing an actual body of knowledge that is critical to human life? How does that realization (or assertion?) affect your desire to study religion?

3. What do you think the minister's primary calling should be? How did you arrive at that conclusion?

4. How would you articulate your own sense of God's calling on your life?

5. How do you see "calling" as synonymous with the opportunity to lead?

6. Practical exercise: In the next few days, take an hour alone with a piece of paper, and write how you perceive God's involvement in your life and calling. How active do you see God's hand in these events and circumstances?.

7. Then list the things you want to accomplish with your life. Write down your dreams, hopes, and desires for your future. Spend some time praying over both your vision for your life and God's unique calling for your vocation.

 **Notes**

1. Nathan O. Hatch, ed., *The Professions in American History* (Notre Dame, IN: University of Notre Dame Press, 1988), 1, 14.

2. See the First Amendment, available at National Archives, "The Charters of Freedom: 'A New World Is at Hand,'" http://www.archives.gov/exhibits/charters/bill_of_rights_transcript.html.

3. See Martin Marty's discussion of the development of the ministerial profession in Hatch, *The Professions in American History*, 75–90.

4. See William H. Willimon, *The Collected Sermons of William H. Willimon* (Louisville: Westminster John Knox, 2010), 56.

5. This practice has a long history. See Keith A. Francis et al., eds., *The Oxford Handbook of the British Sermon* (Oxford: Oxford University Press, 2012), 338.

6. Rees cross-matched differing nations' Quality of Life Index scores, laid over the World Values Survey data, which measure among other things the importance of God in

certain sociological contexts. His conclusions only suggest cause-and-effect relationships but do not substantiate any. His perspective can be found at Tomas Rees, "Non-religious Nations Have Higher Quality of Life," *Epiphenom*, May 13, 2011, http://epiphenom .fieldofscience.com/2011/05/non-religious-nations-have-higher.html.

7. Martin Luther, "To the Christian Nobility of the German Nation Concerning the Reform of the Christian Estate," in *A Reformation Reader: Primary Texts With Introductions,* ed. Denis R. Janz (Minneapolis: Fortress Press, 2002), 98.

8. Dallas Willard, *The Great Omission: Reclaiming Jesus' Essential Teachings on Discipleship* (San Francisco: HarperOne, 2006).

9. See the scene ("I'm Not Alone") on the Yahoo Movies page, https://movies.yahoo .com/video/noah-clip-im-not-alone-154007953.html.

PART

2

Defining Our Praxis

Our discussion of the responsibility of an empowered minister of the gospel brings us to the necessity of understanding a word that recently has come back into good use and effect. That word is *praxis*, and the concept of praxis will help us better understand what ministerial education is geared to achieve. The classical definition of praxis meant reflective action informed by what the ancient Greeks called *phronesus*, or the practical knowledge and skill that enables a person to transform or contextualize (bring up-to-date) a traditional or historically understood meaning of something so it fits into a contemporary context. Praxis is different from "practice," because we rarely reflect on our practices. We simply do our practices without thinking, often out of habit or tradition. Children routinely expose the habitual nature of our practices very simply but eloquently: "Momma, why does the priest wear a white collar?" or "Daddy, is the bread we eat in church really the body of Christ?" Many parents have discovered that they do not know the answers to such questions, yet so often, the tradition continues. Conversely, praxis offers a reflective response to why exactly we engage in certain practices or what they signify. Too often, there is a separation in religious life between action and reflection. Praxis connects action with reflection and communicates a symbiotic, dually informed relationship between the many and varied theories that undergird our practices.[1]

The praxis of mastering the divine is most clearly evident in the ministry capacity when ministers are able to love as they have been loved by God. Agape is a type and quality of love that displays an overarching readiness to seek the goods of human life that are within its range of influence. Agape pursues what is highest and best for the object of its affection. Ministers who lead and guide our congregations, parishes, and churches must seek to understand, embody, and urge the expression of God's agape by the members in and to their world. For what other institution or arena of public life exists that is solely devoted to the spreading of the good news of God's love for the prospering of the general welfare of our world? The church of Jesus Christ alone holds that opportunity. I am not suggesting that all of those in ministry over the past millennia have proven worthy of the dignity their office requires. There have been massive failures regarding praxis, to be sure. These failures have carried dire consequences for the church, which continue to this day. For instance, for centuries now, we have allowed a praxis that marginalizes women in ministry, often treating them as second-class citizens with devastating effects. Furthermore, we have too regularly agreed to disagree disagreeably in innumerable denominational schisms and church splits. This establishes a praxis of discord and disunification. We have allowed consumerism to overwhelm our commitments to the praxis of selfless sacrifice and service to others.

Hence, if the leaders of our local churches are not prepared and focused to make accessible God's wisdom and love, no other group can or will bear such a task. Jesus taught his first-century disciples that agape is the key understanding required for the revolutionary power in his reign as the Messiah, the deliverer, the Son of the living God, to be loosed within the catalytic framework of the church. This has not changed and will not change (Matt. 16:15-19).

Our task here is to investigate the primary subjects that must dominate the interest of professional ministers of the agape of Jesus Christ. To do that, we will engage in the principal pursuit of understanding and then applying Christian theology. This statement is not an attempt to elevate the academic discipline of theology over and above practical ministry or biblical studies. Instead, the thread of theology must be distinctly woven through each of the other disciplines of biblical exegesis, ministerial leadership, spiritual formation, counseling, preaching, and worship. What I want to argue for here is the idea of *theologia*, which has been expertly described by Edward Farley in his classic book *Theologia: The Fragmentation and Unity of Theological Education*.[2] Farley painstakingly walks the reader through the movements of history to describe exactly how theological education and ministerial training have landed on our contemporary doorstep. His conclusion is that *theologia*—which he understands as a holistic embodiment of the knowledge of Christ that leads directly to the manifestation of a Christlike life—has largely disappeared from our contemporary imagination. Instead, we have created a fragmented, disjointed, and isolated approach, resulting in the loss of telos, or purpose, which is the catalyst for theological pursuits.

Farley articulates how the theological academy has slowly created a set of individual, segmented "sciences" and skill development courses that seek only to prepare clergy to run a congregation. That may sound good at first glance. Yet, Farley asks, how would the local church know what it is to do, produce, or achieve, or how is it to define success, if it does not have leaders with enough knowledge of Scripture, church tradition, reason, virtue, and rich experience of God's kingdom to discern and then follow the call of God for its vision? Therefore, Farley believes *theologia*, and not theology, must become the undergirding and unifying thread in every Christian discipline of study.

Let me try to illustrate this point. In biblical studies, instead of only looking for facts or doctrines from the Scriptures, *theologia* encourages us to look for the reasons of God, the revealed truth of God, the purposes of God, and the very thoughts of God as demonstrated in each genre of biblical literature. Within the pages of Scripture, we see how the writers in both testaments have understood and applied God's Word and words in their own lives and contexts, in success and failure, throughout the millennia. Studying the Scriptures is a *theologia* event when students seek to both know and apply an embodiment of the realities of God's kingdom, gathered from the Scriptures. *Theologia* understands the Scriptures as the records of God's word written by disciples for disciples who seek to place their confidence in the character and power of the Most High God.

In contemplating the movements of the church throughout its history, *theologia* provides a means through which to understand what God has done and is doing in and through the *ecclesia*—the called-out and gathered ones, God's church. We see how great thinkers, writers, preachers, and prophets of past eras have understood God, interpreted and applied their understanding of the Scriptures, interacted with one another, and engaged their culture and its principalities and powers. We see how their faith in and conceptions of God have ebbed, flowed, struggled, and grown through success and failure toward increasing degrees of faithfulness to God's call on their lives and societies. Thus, church history is a walk through the evolving lives of the minds and hearts of those who stand shoulder to shoulder with us in our pursuit of *theologia*—the knowledge of Christ—woven in and through the movements of God throughout human history.

Finally, but not least importantly, are the practices we engage in that remind us not only what we believe, but also why we believe what we profess, and what impacts these testimonies have on our daily lives. Our liturgies, whether formal or informal, place the truths we cling to literally before us, calling us toward the eternal hopes we seek to implement in our body, mind, and relationships. When we sing, we put wonderful words, beautiful words into our mouths while simultaneously pulling our longing hearts to experience the realities the words portray. In preaching, we proclaim ideas and opportunities for our lives lived to the fullest in God's good will and kingdom ways. Our ears become trained to hear the good words of God as we listen to God's messages poured over us from the preaching and readings of the Scriptures. In the faithful reception of the Eucharist, we see, feel, taste, and are filled with the mercy, grace, and love of God. The word and sacraments are the tools of God to shape, smooth, heal, and restore the soul so that the mercy, grace, and love of God may in turn flow through us for the good of the world.

This is the telos of *theologia*. If theology is the pursuit of the reasons of God, then *theologia* is the embodiment and manifestation of the effects of that knowledge in our lives. To have only one is to not have the other. Therefore, the goal and necessity of the minister of Christ is to attain a mastery of *theologia*, not just theology, history, Scripture, and practical ministry. To miss the former is to risk ignorance of the primary mission of God for humanity. Therefore, *theologia* must remain the sole objective of the teaching institutions seeking to disciple ministers of the gospel of Jesus Christ, as well. This book series is an excellent introduction to each of these distinct and invaluable areas of God's unique and wondrous works that together lead us into an experience of the knowledge of God. Together they create the means of entering eternal life (John 17:3).

Five Praxes That Define Ministerial Life

As the following books in this series will more completely investigate, the professional minister has the opportunity to follow the movements of God through several key areas and disciplines of study. This first book introduces five primary themes or pillars on which the larger concept of *theologia* will rest within each of the disciplines that follow. For *theologia* to take hold in the hearts and minds of professional Christian ministers, these five areas of special knowledge, essential to the common good, are areas to be properly mastered, and ministers should be held accountable for them by their peers. It stands to reason that these key areas are also the most important aspects of human life. The first area relates to the essence of what it means to have a spiritual nature and live a spiritual life. The second area is connected to the life and function of the thoughts and ideas that fill our minds. The third area concerns how the spiritual life, combined with the mental life, comes to inhabit our bodies and direct our behaviors. Fourth is the nature of community, our relationships with others, and fitting together the distinct members of the body of Christ into his church. Finally, and perhaps most overlooked, is the minister's leadership of others in guiding the local church.

At first glance, these objectives may not strike future ministers as the primary means through which Christian ministry should be approached. However, special knowledge is not to be confused with "secret knowledge" or some sense of mysticism. Instead, ministers of the gospel must become experts in recognizing the power intrinsic to the ideas and thoughts we carry and dwell upon, in combination with the invisible qualities and characteristics of both human existence and the divine nature of God and God's kingdom. When this occurs, this spiritual power and the knowledge of God must become embodied in our habits and practices. Finally, we can consider each of these aspects of ideology, spirituality, embodiment, and relationality when conjoined with and directed toward the purposes God has for the church. Putting all of these aspects together as a leader is the ultimate and highest calling of a Christian minister. For it is when the truth and power of the church are unleashed into our communities that the good news can begin to transform the kingdoms of our world into the kingdom of God and of his Christ, which will reign forever and ever. Amen.

Each of these aspects of human life and living has been significantly marginalized in recent decades. The minister's task is to provide the means for reestablishing confidence in the entirety of Jesus' good news that touches every aspect of human existence. When the gospel is universally applied, both individually and collectively, no other means of life and living demonstrates both the power and confidence to transform the spiritual and material realities of our world. Thus, the minister's primary objective is to master each of these areas of praxis through study, reflection, and application.

 ## Questions for Exploration

1. What are some of the unconscious or assumed religious practices or beliefs that have become traditions or habits in your life that may need reconsideration?

2. What are some of the more controversial applications of praxis that have directly affected your journey of faith? Are you interested in learning more about these ideas, their origins, and others who have engaged these ideas?

3. Of the people you have known in your life, who has mastered the divine in the way it is described here?

4. Which of the great Christians throughout church history have inspired and encouraged you?

5. Do you know where your praxis comes from and when it started?

6. Do you want to?

 **Notes**

1. This was the understanding of praxis in Habermas, Tracy, and Fowler. See Jürgen Habermas, *Theory and Practice* (London: Heinemann, 1974); David Tracy, *Blessed Rage for Order: The New Pluralism in Theology, with a New Preface* (Chicago: University of Chicago Press, 1996), 244; James W. Fowler, *Faith Development and Pastoral Care* (Philadelphia: Fortress Press, 1987), 15–16.

2. Edward Farley, *Theologia: The Fragmentation and Unity of Theological Education* (Minneapolis: Fortress Press, 1983).

Praxis One:
The Spiritual Life

We start our study of praxes by considering the spiritual life. This should be a fairly simple task, but over the past several centuries, the very concept of spirituality has been routinely dashed on the rocks of rationalism, naturalism, and scientism. Therefore, although spirituality is the bread-and-butter reality underlying the Christian life, fewer and fewer people, even within the Christian community, have been exposed to a clear understanding or education regarding the spiritual life.

We see this same problem and its effect on poor Nicodemus, whose fateful evening meeting with Jesus on the rooftop was very difficult for him to comprehend. Contrary to Nicodemus's religious upbringing, Jesus was trying to introduce him to the spiritual life (John 3). Although confused at first, Nicodemus was able to grasp an understanding of the spiritual life and appears to have overcome his obstacles in a fairly short period of time (John 7:45-51; 19:39-42). The key point to understand is Jesus believed that Nicodemus, as a teacher of the law or even a rabbi like himself, should have understood the nature of and the difference between the things of the spirit and those of the physical world. Jesus gives a gentle but clear rebuke to Nicodemus, holding him to account for his lack of understanding of such crucial matters of religious life (John 3:10). In fact, this was something Nicodemus could have known, as it was a significant part of the teachings of the Jewish Scriptures available to him.

The same is true for ministers today. God's first and chief attribute is God's spiritual nature. We often forget that God is spirit (John 4:24), something Nicodemus struggled to understand and apply to his own theology. God's spiritual nature means God is invisible, without a physical representation or body. Yet this does not mean God is any less personal or powerful. Our struggle to engage in the spiritual nature of our own lives often hinders our life with God. How we conceive of spirituality will by and large direct the degree to which we can encounter the blessings of God and God's kingdom. This remains something of a hurdle and mystery in Christian life and is one piece of evidence we should consider in thinking about what ministers of *theologia* should experience in their own lives, and how, in order to be qualified to teach others.

We often call this spiritual formation, but a more accurate and helpful description may be to think about the *transformation* of our spiritual lives, since many of us have received a great deal of formation already. Therefore, we must be, as Paul so accurately described, transformed by the renewing of our minds (Rom. 12:2). I suggest that this transformation, following renewal, comes from reconsidering who we believe or know God to be—again, a key tenet of *theologia*.

The apostle Paul argues in Romans 1 that we are obligated to know God, and ignorance about God is the main cause of human suffering. If we took this seriously, we would spend much more of our time and treasure making sure we have an accurate conception of God and God's nature. Of course, this is precisely what Christian education has attempted to prioritize in its more effective eras. Paul states, "For what can be known about God is plain to them, because God has shown it to them. Ever since the creation of the world his eternal power and divine nature, invisible though they are, have been understood and seen through the things he has made. So they are without excuse; for though they knew God, they did not honor him as God or give thanks to him, but they became futile in their thinking, and their senseless minds were darkened" (1:19–21 NRSV).

Paul's observation of the first century is still emblematic of our contemporary condition. God is not hiding. God desires to be known and has revealed his will, character, essence, and ways through various means, or as Psalm 8 describes them, through the "works of his hands" (v6, NKJV). These works are unavoidably enormous. It doesn't take too much reflection to sense the sheer immensity and omnipotence of God by looking at the world itself. Just the physical creation alone has enabled many "nonbelievers" to begin a journey down the path of seeking God. The physical, material creation almost instinctively leads the mind and heart toward a sense of awe that longs to be filled (Heb. 11:3).

Here, we can only tap the surface on the nature of God, but *theologia* begins with a thoughtful reflection on the total object of our devotions. Theologian Adam Clark helps us to grasp a somewhat bigger view of the God we seek to know, love, and serve:

> The eternal, independent and self-existent Being; the Being whose purposes and actions spring from himself, without foreign motive or influence; he who is absolute in dominion; the most pure, the most simple, the most spiritual of all essences; infinitely perfect; and eternally self-sufficient, needing nothing that he has made; illimitable in his immensity, inconceivable in his mode of existence, and indescribable in his essence; known fully only to himself, because an infinite mind can only be fully comprehended by itself. In a word, a being who from his infinite wisdom, cannot err or be deceived and who from his infinite goodness can do nothing but what is eternally just and right and kind.[1]

The type of deity Clark introduces is one that might more fully fill our imaginations and stir a level of devotion that will motivate ministers of the gospel to faithfully steward their calling well. This is *theologia* at its best. Out of goodwill and agape love that flows effortlessly from God's self, God acted and created the material universe that surrounds us. In this knowledge, we discover the immense amount of power at God's command. We can even connect this to one of the most amazing discoveries in the modern sciences, commonly known as $E = mc^2$. In light of God's creative potency, we realize that matter is full of energy, the energy that originates from the willing Spirit of an infinitely creative God. Even the tiniest particles of matter contain immense amounts of power, to such a magnitude that when an atom is split, the power released is almost unfathomable. This shows that God's creative energy, not matter alone, lies at the foundation of our world. In the beginning, God. This is the power that Noah recognized was worthy of his life and faith.

Similarly, Jesus' miracles not only demonstrated his divinity, but also revealed his mastery of the spiritual realities that undergird all physical realities. His supernatural works stemmed from a complete understanding of the nature of God's being, the workings of God's kingdom, and the purposes to which God's power was to be directed. Each is an invisible, nonmaterial, spiritual reality. Connection to these makes living in and through the Spirit of God possible. This is what Jesus endeavored to teach his first followers and what *theologia* aims to achieve: a knowledge of God that empowers a minister to accomplish the will of God, just as Christ demonstrated and then charged his disciples to achieve as well (Matt. 28:19-20).

God has given humanity dominion over God's creation. As a result, we are to steward and protect all creation. God has also given us the power to control and direct our own bodies, in order to steward the creation well. In this co-creative relationship, God has also allowed us the great privilege of working with God to create other persons, our children. As we work in concert with God and utilize our minds, bodies, and relationships, God's power in us reflects God's image. We have the opportunity to decide how we will direct the freedom of our will. Therefore, our spirits or wills have been formed and are in constant need of transformation. When we intend to be conformed, and therefore transformed, into the image of Christ, God empowers us to do God's will, which is continually becoming our will. This is the power-sharing intention of God from the beginning of creation and is the final objective of God's purposes in eternity. The goal of learning from Jesus how to live is directly conjoined with the training required for knowing and then doing God's will. This is identical to the way Jesus wielded God's power.

Yet we can easily see how such power could be misused, as well, if placed in the wrong hands. Great power requires great responsibility; therefore, power cannot be entrusted to individuals ill equipped to accomplish good ends. This is Jesus' goal in discipleship and likewise the primary responsibility of the church in developing disciples. A church is where disciples are developed to appropriately handle the awesome responsibilities of power. In this way, Paul reveals churches, which are comprised of disciples, will be able to defer to one another in mutual submission, not out of obligation or authoritative power plays due to position or prestige, but out of love and respect:

> So if there is any encouragement in Christ, any comfort from love, any participation in the Spirit, any affection and sympathy, complete my joy by being of the same mind, having the same love, being in full accord and of one mind. Do nothing from selfish ambition or conceit, but in humility count others more significant than yourselves. Let each of you look not only to his own interests, but also to the interests of others. Have this mind among yourselves, which is yours in Christ Jesus, who, though he was in the form of God, did not count equality with God a thing to be grasped, but emptied himself, by taking the form of a servant, being born in the likeness of men. And being found in human form, he humbled himself by becoming obedient to the point of death, even death on a cross. Therefore God has highly exalted him and bestowed on him the name that is above every name, so that at the name of Jesus every knee should bow, in heaven and on earth and under the earth, and every tongue confess that Jesus Christ is Lord, to the glory of God the Father.
>
> Therefore, my beloved, as you have always obeyed, so now, not only as in my presence but much more in my absence, work out your own salvation with fear and trembling, for it is God who works in you, both to will and to work for his good pleasure.
>
> Do all things without grumbling or disputing, that you may be blameless and innocent, children of God without blemish in the midst of a crooked and twisted generation, among whom you shine as lights in the world. (Phil. 2:1-15 ESV)

We struggle with the gap between what we intend and what we accomplish. Intentional discipleship to Jesus could bridge the divide between the nature of God as spirit, the invisible power available in God's kingdom, and the effects of God's love in our everyday lives, each of which must first become a clear articulation of the gospel firmly established in our minds. When our minds are renewed to these realities, we can begin the transformation into the children of light Paul speaks of.

We are infinite spiritual beings with a destiny to live with God and others and enjoy the universe God designed for us. If the church and its leaders remain unaware of this, we have little opportunity to make transformative improvements that can revolutionize our lives, causing our heart, soul, mind, and strength to grow in love for God and others with the same love God gives us.

This is the manifestation of *theologia* that must start with our professional ministers and therefore has to be a major focal point in our theological institutions and seminaries. Where else is the knowledge and experience of the spiritual life to be gained? Where else are these kinds of people trained to pursue these sorts of values and realities? Yes, our seminaries and schools of theology are the only institutions wherein these ideas and virtues are intensely pursued and ingrained. There simply is no substitute or alternative. This intricate and invaluable experience with the spiritual essence of life with God is the purpose behind the creation of institutions pursuing *theologia*. And the whole earth groans as it waits for the knowledge of God to be displayed in and through God's children (Rom. 8:19).

I'll never forget the first time I witnessed my oldest daughter on horseback. I spent most of that initial hour-long lesson completely on edge. It was just about all I could do to not jump the rail of the corral and pull her out of the saddle. She looked so tiny on top of that mammoth animal, so unstable, and a little afraid. She had no control over the horse; I knew it, she knew it, the trainer knew it, and maybe even the horse knew it. But the look on her face told me all I needed to know. She was hooked, and for the next several years that have followed, she has invested nearly every spare moment in a barn or corral. She has logged thousands of hours with horses, washing them down, grooming, cleaning hooves, mucking stalls, and riding. She often comes home exhausted, dirty, smelly, sore, hungry, and utterly content. She has found her place in the world. There is no smile on her face like the smile she carries after a great ride.

Now, some seven years later, after my daughter has spent thousands of hours practicing and developing her knowledge of the equestrian trade, it's a marvel to watch her at a horse show. Her bedroom now bears tribute to her growing mastery, with multicolored ribbons cascading over her walls. She has learned exactly how to lead, command, and discipline the horse to do precisely what she desires. They work together as one, the animal an extension of her will. Just a slight movement of the weight, a slight bit of pressure with the reins, a whisper in the ear, and a 1,200-pound mass of lean muscle and power caters to every command. All those hours of practice, care, tending, and affection have allowed my daughter to develop a bond, a connection with these horses that transcends the physical training alone. There is a smooth effortlessness, a dance really, in the combination of her direction and the horse's response. This is a wonderful image of the spiritual life: Two wills intertwined into one motion. The spiritual directing the physical toward something neither would achieve on its own. Teamwork, partnership, submission, and respect for the gifts given and received one with the other.

Christian spirituality is the source of our power, for the Holy Spirit is the power for the Christian life. Learning to know God and who we are as God's children, created as both spiritual and physical beings representing our creator's image, propels us toward the transformation required for us to be worthy students of Jesus who can be empowered by the Holy Spirit to accomplish God's mission in our world. Such a transformation is what *theologia* intends, and it provides for us a bracket from which we can understand the overarching purposes for Christian ministers and their education. Knowing God, knowing the self, and navigating the gap in our knowledge of both, through God's love in order to achieve God's purposes by God's empowered grace—these form the basis of all Christian work. These were Jesus' objectives in his earthly ministry, and they remain ours as well. Because of Jesus' work, we now stand poised to engage God and God's power for accomplishing God's will, which Paul reminds us is abundantly more than anyone could hope or imagine (Eph. 3:20). *Theologia* education directs ministers to the source of spiritual power that is absolutely sufficient to their calling. Therefore, our mastery of these foundational concepts, followed by our faithful communication of *theologia* and our modeling of the spiritual life infused by this *theologia*, is essential if our ministries are to impact the world for good.

Questions for Exploration

1. How does *theologia* represent itself in your life?
2. What do you think about the definition of God offered by Adam Clark? Does that represent or miss your understanding of the nature of God? Why? Have you ever thought about God in these types of terms?
3. What do you think is more powerful in your life: the physical or the spiritual aspect of your nature?
4. What are the invisible aspects of your life that you appreciate the most?
5. The chapter argues that the church is to be a place where disciples learn how to wield the power of God for God's purposes. Do you agree? Why or why not? What is your expectation or experience of your current church setting?

Notes

1. Adam Clark, "Definition of God," in *Cyclopedia of Biblical, Theological and Ecclesiastical Literature*, ed. John McClintock and James Strong (New York: Harper, 1894), 903–904.

Praxis Two: A Life of Meditation and Contemplation

In concert with the life in the Spirit, the life of meditation and contemplation represents the second essential tool that professional Christian ministers must learn to use and use well. We can call these skills part and parcel of a life devoted to the development of the mind. What we fill our minds with, what our thoughts dwell upon, is of primary importance in the development of who we become as human beings. Likewise, what we think about is an area of human life that requires significant attention for ministers of the gospel.

As perhaps is already obvious, much of what has been discussed thus far dwells in the realm of ideas. Oddly enough, most of us were introduced to the gospel as a set of ideas, especially if we first encountered Jesus' teaching as adults. Before we made a decision about the truthfulness or reliability of the message of the gospel, we first grasped each of the ideas inside the story represented through the Bible as a collection of ordered proposals that profess a certain conclusion or worldview. And before a decision can be made regarding any conclusion from a proposal presented as a result of tying a set of ideas together in certain ways, we have to make sense of them, sometimes individually, sometimes as a whole. For some, this process of assimilation and reasoning must be done in some kind of order, perhaps one by one. For others, the big picture is enough, and the details can follow as needed, if at all. Still, few ever reach complete mastery of all the ideas connected to the message of Jesus or the story of Scripture. However, some level of understanding is necessary in order to justify any decision required for meaningful action.

In commenting on Prov. 23:7 ("For as he thinks within himself, so he is," NASB), A. W. Tozer has stated, "What comes into our minds when we think about God indeed is the most important thing about us!"[1] Besides our priests and pastors, no other position in our society today has the opportunity and responsibility to represent, teach, train, and guide others' thoughts toward God in good and appropriate ways. Their ability or inability to properly direct our thoughts toward God and shape how we think and act toward our neighbors, our enemies, and even our own existence will dramatically influence our societies and our world. This is primarily why it was thought beneficial to print sermons in local newspapers. How we think leads to how we act and what we live for. Knowledge of God has dramatic repercussions on such vital issues. Such an idea itself is in jeopardy today, both inside and outside our churches. Still, Paul was well aware of the crucial truth Tozer illuminates. Romans 1 reveals the trajectory of human existence when the thoughts and ideas of God become lost or inconsequential within either the individual mind or the collective human consciousness. What becomes of us when God is lost to our minds isn't a pretty picture.

Who is God, and how do we come to know God? These are the ominous questions that continuously hover over an increasingly secular society. This is why preaching and teaching, as events intended to transfer the knowledge of God, are so unequivocally necessary for the common well-being. The preaching and teaching of the knowledge of God reveals the nature of God's existence, as well as God's will and ways. In its most basic form, the gospel of Jesus Christ consists of the real, true, and beautiful knowledge of, from, and about God. For humanity to understand and live in Jesus' message of whole life, life to the full, we must begin to place our minds in its fullness (John 10:10 NIV). Hence, attempts to reduce or "dumb down" the gospel to only a few crucial doctrines or beliefs runs the risk of highlighting the marginal while missing the core. The gospel is larger and more effectual than what occurred during a few hours on the cross or what might happen at the end of human history. Such beliefs, as important as they are, if allowed to become the primary considerations on which we dwell in our thoughts and beliefs about our faith, can cause us to miss the entirety of God's objectives for the whole of creation. We could even risk missing God entirely. The gospel of Jesus offer us a life now, right where we are, in our everyday, go-to-work, come-home-from-school, feed-the-dog sort of life. The life Jesus offers us is eternal, meaning unlimited in both quality and quantity. To be eternal is to have no end, in either time or substance. It means to be full, to overflow the barriers, spilling over onto others who have the blessing of being in our company and receiving the goodness with which God has blessed our lives (Luke 6:38).

Missing the opportunity to attain this knowledge of God and God's plentitude is perhaps some of what Paul is warning the Christians in Ephesus against:

> Now this I affirm and insist on in the Lord: you must no longer live as the Gentiles live, in the futility of their minds. They are darkened in their understanding, alienated from the life of God because of their ignorance and hardness of heart. They have lost all sensitivity and have abandoned themselves to licentiousness, greedy to practice every kind of impurity. That is not the way you learned Christ! For surely you have heard about him and were taught in him, as truth is in Jesus. You were taught to put away your former way of life, your old self, corrupt and deluded by its lusts, and to be renewed in the spirit of your minds, and to clothe yourselves with the new self, created according to the likeness of God in true righteousness and holiness. (Eph. 4:17-24)

Pay special attention to some of the terms Paul uses in this passage: "futility of their minds," "darkened in their understanding," "ignorance," "learned," "taught," and "truth." These words and phrases relate to the life of the mind.

The mind becomes dark when it is alienated from the light of God, which, according to Jesus' sermon on the mountain, Christians are to embody and share with the entire world. We are to be, and point to, the Light of the world. Therefore, the local congregation is intended to be the primary spot where this light of truth and love is ignited, tended, and grown to be sent out into the world; in this way, the church acts as a shining city on top of a hill—a sight that cannot be missed (Matt. 5:14).

Lastly, it is through our minds that we make contact, not only with the world around us, but also with God. God is a part of our world, our cosmos, and we engage God primarily through our minds. There is nothing overtly magical or mysterious about this. We make contact with all the sources of power in the universe through our minds. Therefore, if we fail to utilize our ability to turn our minds and thoughts toward God, we will miss God as well. This is why Moses encouraged his mentee, Joshua, to meditate on God's word day and night, keeping God's decrees and truth on his lips, chewing on it as a substance, for that is exactly what it is (Josh. 1:8). Therefore, we, too, can get to the point where we consciously and intentionally focus our minds on God. The professional minister of the gospel is tasked with the very special and essential job of illuminating our minds and guiding them toward the realities of God in ways that inspire, rebuke, correct, and encourage us to increasingly place our confidence in the character of the Good Shepherd.

Hopefully, we can now see how closely the life of the mind falls in line with the objectives of a course of study directed toward *theologia*. Together, a life dependent upon and utilizing the power of God's spirit and a life devoted to meditating on and contemplating the things of God are the stones necessary for building a sturdy foundation on which the primary pursuits within the ministerial profession are laid. The specific fields of history, doctrine, preaching, biblical interpretation, leadership, etc. will appropriately fall between these two principal abilities within Christian spirituality and contemplation. When they are effectively merged into our educational institutions, ministry students will become equipped to navigate the transcendent knowledge of God and God's character, along with the more visceral responsibilities to lead themselves and others toward God's wisdom in the many trying situations of contemporary life.

The knowledge and experience of the divine nature, and a life given to study, reflection, and contemplation of God and God's ways in a manner that transforms the character, give any minister of Christ a form of authority that is desperately needed and currently missing in our society. We have excellent examples of ministers, such as Dietrich Bonhoeffer, Martin Luther King Jr., Mother Teresa, and Desmond Tutu, who wonderfully depict lives devoted to both the mind and the spirit, which carried them into specific areas of study and service. Their mastery of these two critical arenas of ministerial life forged a credibility that transcended the cultural resistance to their claims.[2] This is the calling and expectation of a minister of the gospel of Jesus Christ. And the world longs for these sons and daughters of the King to take their rightful place among us. This is one of the primary objectives of a life devoted to *theologia.*

A very dear mentor of mine used to remind me that the genesis of Adolf Hitler's and Pol Pot's ideologies were developed not in war rooms or political capitals but in the breeding grounds of the intellectually sophisticated café cultures of Paris and Vienna.[3] It was in the intellectual repose of ideological hotbeds where these minds began to incubate schemes that would culminate in the commission of the two most heinous crimes against humanity in the last century. If such indescribable evil can be hatched as a result of one's devotion to the intellectual life, so too can unfathomable goodness. Paris and Vienna have also inspired greater minds like Voltaire, Jean-Jacques Rousseau, Victor Hugo, Wolfgang Amadeus Mozart, and Ludwig van Beethoven. What is the difference? I suggest the difference is not found in the coffee but rather in what these minds are set upon and what they intend to do with the thoughts that fill their minds. Proper thinking is a significant aspect of the calling of the professional minister and the challenge of appropriate training of our professional ministers in the seminary setting. Theological education must remain committed to students who desire to fill their minds, and the minds of others, with the wonders and power of God's truth, seeking to inspire not fear but confidence and commitment in congregants and parishioners who become blessed by the ideas their words convey and the truths their characters manifest.

 Questions for Exploration

1. What attracts you, or what causes you to struggle with a life of thoughtful contemplation?
2. Is there anything that concerns you about considering the ministry as being devoted equally to thoughtfulness, meditation, and reflective study on the one hand and to more outward activities, such as service projects, visiting the sick, or feeding the hungry, on the other? Are these two praxes mutually exclusive? Why or why not? How might they be complementary?
3. Do you ever feel a degree of intimidation when thinking about studying the nature of God? For some, the study of God's nature can seem unending and unfathomable. Do you ever have similar thoughts? Explain.
4. What are the ideas about God or God's ways that you would most like to seek answers for? Why do you think these are the questions you are most interested in?

 Notes

1. A. W. Tozer, *The Knowledge of the Holy: The Attributes of God; Their Meaning in the Christian Life* (San Francisco: HarperSanFrancisco, 1992), 1.

2. Great references to start reading about these key figures and their life of devotion to the mind and spirit are Eric Metaxas, *Bonhoeffer: Pastor, Martyr, Prophet, Spy; A Righteous Gentile vs. The Third Reich* (Nashville: Thomas Nelson, 2010); Kathryn Spink, *Mother Teresa: A Complete Authorized Biography*, rev. ed. (New York: HarperOne, 2011); Desmond Tutu, *An African Prayer Book* (New York: Doubleday, 1995); Wright L. Lassiter Jr., *The Power of Thought: A Series of Messages Celebrating the Life of Dr. Martin Luther*

King, Jr. (Bloomington, IN: Trafford, 2011); Rufus Burrow, *Martin Luther King Jr., Man of Ideas and Nonviolent Social Action* (Minneapolis: Fortress Press, 2014); José Luis González-Balado, *Teresa of Calcutta: A Personal Memoir* (Liguori, MO: Liguori, 2007); Martin Luther King Jr., *The Measure of a Man* (Minneapolis: Fortress Press, 2001).

3. James Tyner, *War Violence and Population: Making the Body Count* (New York: Guilford, 2009), 117–18, 203–204ff; and Brigitte Hamann, *Hitler's Vienna: A Dictator's Apprenticeship* (New York: Oxford University Press, 1999), 140–41.

Praxis Three:
An Embodied Faith

After we understand that our Christian life is one devoted to spiritual realities and we become aware of the crucial exercise of intentionally placing our minds on the things of God and God's kingdom, Christian ministers then must be able to demonstrate in their own lives and teach others how the Spirit of God joins with our individual spirit to guide and direct our thoughts, beliefs, actions, and attitudes. All of this occurs inside and then through our bodies. To leave Christian faith at the level of ideas and the transcendent beliefs about things pertaining to only the spiritual, while leaving our bodies to fend for themselves, is to make the gravest of errors in discerning exactly what Jesus intended for his first disciples. It was both their beliefs and behaviors that became habituated in their bodies that Jesus knew must come under the grace and power of God in order for a life to be transformed and to abide in God's kingdom. Therefore, ministers of the gospel must also take seriously the means God has provided for the transformation of our bodies to work in concert with the transformation of our spirit and mind.

Today, much of Christianity is concerned with and devoted to doctrine and tradition. These are very good areas of Christian life to which we should pay a good amount of our time and attention. For instance, the ideas of the forgiveness of sin, the means of God's grace, and the awareness of God's truth are key to the life of a maturing disciple. Furthermore, our engagements with God in personal, intimate ways within our services, such as through listening to an inspired sermon or in the practice of our liturgies (Eucharist, baptism, etc.), are all valuable means of growing our faith. Yet the application of spiritual disciplines—of which attending worship services can be one form of discipline—should rise to equal importance in our thinking, praxis, and leadership for one very straightforward reason. Without the application of spiritual disciplines, our liturgies, rituals, and sermonizing will not produce large numbers of disciples, only consumers of religious goods and services. Again, Dallas Willard has pointedly realized that, in the absence of actually reforming our habits through the disciplines, our churches will not "reliably produce large numbers of people who really are like Christ and his closest followers throughout history."[1] Without intentionally applying various disciplines, Christians will never move from imitating actors on a stage who profess ideas about what ought to be but never demonstrate what has become actualized in our real lives as a result of living in the reality of God's kingdom.

And here lies the crux of the matter. The nonbelieving world rarely, if ever, resists the Christian ideals of love, peace, patience, kindness, gentleness, faith, hope, and forgiveness. The most significant critique of contemporary Christianity stems from the unfaithfulness we Christians portray to the very message we proclaim. Simply put, the number of people actually transformed by the gospel appears to be far smaller than the number who profess its truth and power. The discrepancy is deadly to the credibility of the message itself. A "do as I say and not as I do" methodology is deadly to the gospel. This Jesus knew very well and highlighted in the first century regarding the religious hypocrisy of the Pharisees (Matt. 5:20). The gospel, if left disembodied, is easily dismissed as pie-in-the-sky positive thinking at best and psychological delusion at worst. We must take seriously the opportunity and responsibility to bring our actual lives, which don't get any more concrete than our physical bodies, into the practice of our faith. It is only when we make our bodies subject *to* our faith and our bodies become transformed by the power *of* our faith that we are able, as Paul commands, to "mortify the deeds of the body" (Rom. 8:13 KJV) and follow his instructions to "exercise thyself unto godliness" (Rom. 5:2 ASV) as all exercises are done: by offering our "present your bodies a living sacrifice, holy, acceptable to God, which is your spiritual service." (Rom. 12:1 ASV).

So what are these disciplines, and why are they so crucial to the life of the minister? First, we want to point out that living the life of a disciple and modeling that life as a minister to others assumes a level of conformity, learning, and modeling one's own life to the life Jesus lived in his flesh. And it may be news to some, but Jesus is seen routinely practicing spiritual disciplines during his ministry. Certainly, not all the spiritual disciplines are strictly somatic, or bodily. But many are, and the overwhelming majority— say, meditation and prayer—require the body to work with the will if these disciplines are going to work well. Thus, the primary point to understand is that to live in a Christlike way directly assumes there is a devotion to do the things and practice the practices that Jesus did and practiced. Such a statement may seem so simple as to be overtly obvious, but the lack of conformity to this fact makes it more obvious that Christians seem unaware of this basic understanding. Rarely do we hear or see those in our churches or those leading our congregations acknowledging or teaching about the disciplines Jesus practiced. This must change if we are to reasonably expect our churches to change. Therefore, change must begin with our leaders who meet and dwell with Christ, learning to reshape their lives into his image, by his grace and power, in the disciplines of the spiritual life.

What are the disciplines Jesus practiced? Silence, solitude, fasting, prayer, fellowship, meditation, worship, secrecy, giving, study, celebration, service, simplicity, Scripture memorization, and suffering are but a few of the examples we have noted in the gospel accounts. The primary point is that we can become apprentices, disciples of Jesus, through applying the means he applied to his own life and body while placing his confidence in God and God's grace to empower him to do what he needed to do in and through his calling. The minister of the gospel is called to embody the same life and the same vision. There is no other means of embodying the life of Christ than to practice the disciplines he practiced with the intent of becoming the kind of person he was, who knew what he knew, believed what he believed, and therefore acted as he acted. The great secret Jesus knew and longed to share with others is that a disciplined life is an easy life, a good life, free from the burdens that so easily entangle us. We do this by entering Jesus' yoke, his teaching device, where we learn of him and his gentle means of instruction, wherein rest and peace are found (Matt. 29:30). This yoke is entered through the spiritual disciplines. Therefore, our professional ministers must be trained in the disciplines, to employ them and teach others how and why to follow their lead.

The result? Christlikeness. How? After practicing the discipline of silence, we learn how to tune our ear to God's quiet, noncompeting voice. We also learn to shut the mouth, to not speak when silence is the better alternative, to not trust words as the only means of moving our world and those around us. In solitude, we learn to wean ourselves from dependent relationships that tempt us into placing our confidence for our success or survival on certain key people of influence over and above God's mighty hand in our lives. Solitude allows us to realize that our reputation need not be our primary concern, that God can and will elevate us as is appropriate and necessary for our calling. In solitude, we are freed from the need to have people fill our sense of significance, and thus we become increasingly able to love unconditionally, without requiring a return investment of devotion for the relationships we seek.

Prayer and meditation allow our minds to contemplate the things of God and God's work in our lives and ministries in order to align our often-misaligned vision for our lives. Prayer is God's power-sharing and action-directing means of communication. However, prayer requires listening much more than speaking. Listening is a skill that needs developing, along with the training of the mind to focus for extended periods of time on key issues without distraction. This can be done, but like any skill, whether learning to play the piano or mastering a foreign language, prayer and meditation require time, devotion, and the direct application of a will to achieve a desired end. The spiritual discipline of study offers a similar effect.

The final example we will engage here is the discipline of fellowship. Unlike in solitude, where we remove ourselves from the company of others, in fellowship, we intentionally place ourselves in the company of others. We learn to listen, to be patient, and to share our lives, our loves, our hurts, and our celebrations with others. For some, perhaps those who tend to be more extroverted, such a discipline may seem easy and enjoyable. Instead, for "people persons," engaging the discipline of fellowship may require pulling back from the spotlight or resisting the need to become the center of attention when in the company of others. However, for those who are shy or introverted, the discipline may be more crucial and revolutionary. Introverts can become closed off from the benefits of belonging to a larger community and begin to wonder what profit is gained from the company of others. Yet, in fellowship, we experience the synergy of God's power united in the collected body of Christ. In that way, we learn to be appropriately sustained by God's provision given for us through others. Redemption and renewal of our hearts, minds, and bodies is not a solitary thing but involves a flood of countless individual participants sharing in God's bountiful blessings, which are simultaneously individual and communal. When I am blessed by God, others are blessed as well. These blessings can be shared only when we gather to share them. This is one of the primary benefits of communal fellowship of the saints.

The primary point to remember is that each of these disciplines is irreducibly bodily. I shut my actual mouth in silence and seek to avoid noise that normally fills my ears. I place my body and person in a solitary place, away from other people, in the discipline of solitude. With my hands, I pick up the Scriptures or a text and sit my body down for extended periods in a chair, focusing my eyes on the pages in order to read the words on the page when I study. I also focus my mind, training it to think new thoughts and follow lines of reasoning of others in the texts I study. I also consider new possibilities or changes that might occur in the circumstances of my life, given the new ideas I encounter. In fellowship, I place my body and person in the company of others, engaging in conversation, listening, laughing, celebrating, remembering, or weeping with them as the situation dictates. I listen to the stories of the lives of others, and I learn to understand and tell my own story, hearkening to encounters with the movements of God in our midst.

These disciplines are a few of the means of grace that Jesus used to engage in the spiritual life with God and with those around him. And in these practices, Jesus manifested the power and profundity of God's kingdom way, experiencing it for himself and manifesting it to others, while testifying to its many benefits. This was possible because God's goodness, power, and love resided in him. They were in his mind, in his spirit, and in his body. He could keep silent in front of the Sanhedrin; he could turn the other cheek as Roman guards slapped him; he could kiss Judas, his betrayer, with his lips; he could wash his friends' feet; "when they hurled their insults at him he did not retaliate: when he suffered, he made no threats. Instead, he entrusted himself to him who judges justly" (1 Pet. 2:23 NIV). All of this he was able to do because love was in him and hate was not in him. The love and assurance of God were visibly, physically embodied in his heart, mind, hands, face, eyes, and lips and shone through in his actions, attitudes, and relationships with others. This is the embodied life of Christ that ministers of the gospel of Jesus can take seriously and learn diligently if they are to model the calling Jesus exemplified for those who carry his name.

Questions for Exploration

1. What experience or history do you have with the spiritual disciplines?
2. What ways have you found that help you to embody your faith? What practices are not helpful and why?
3. Do you consider study, contemplation, church attendance, Bible reading, and prayer spiritual disciplines? If not, why? If so, what are the embodied results you have discovered as a result of practicing these disciplines?

4. Think about all the disciplines Jesus practiced. Why do you think he practiced these disciplines? Do you think the same regimen he used is beneficial for us? Why or why not?

 Notes

1. Dallas Willard, *The Spirit of the Disciplines: Understanding How God Changes Lives* (San Francisco: HarperOne, 1991), preface.

Praxis Four: Life Together in the Flock of the Good Shepherd

After discussing how the life of the spirit, the mind, and the body are crucial to development of a minister of the gospel, we must now consider how these personal or individual aspects of discipleship conjoin with the overall direction and purposes of the church. I believe in the church, the body of Christ, who is its creator and prime sustainer. Therefore, I also believe in the power of God to work in and through our pastors and priests as they prepare to accomplish the calling of serving Christ as he builds his church. Likewise, the authors that follow in this book series will describe in more detail how the work of ministry leaders, spokespersons, and teachers can understand and describe the nature and "reasonings" (*logia*) of God (*theo*) as a loving, attentive, present, protective, and providing Shepherd in every aspect of human life in and through his *ecclesia*, his "called-out ones," his church. Living in, testifying to, and demonstrating the effects of the power and blessing of life in Jesus' flock is the primary purpose of Jesus' church, and we should remember to hold ourselves to account for measuring the fruit of abiding in Christ as the vine. Only Christ—and nothing, or no one, else—causes us to bear the fruit of his Spirit. Jesus describes this type of life in John 17:3 NASB: "This is eternal life, that they may know You, the only true God, and Jesus Christ whom You have sent." To truly know the Shepherd is to have life that never ends, life that is limitless in time and quality.

Therefore, the first and most crucial task for our churches is to be led by professional ministers who know—read that again: *know*—God as their own shepherd. An intimate awareness of the Psalm 23 kind of life must precede all of our grand and important endeavors to build churches, develop ministry programs, preach sermons, or write texts. The primary role of professional ministers is not to build temples, manage real estate portfolios, raise money, or promote programs to attract religious consumers. As good as each of these activities of our churches might be in itself, the primary and essential task of ministers leading our churches is to teach, preach, and manifest, first in their own lives, and then through their ministries, the power and truth available for all of life and living contained within the knowledge of God and life in God's kingdom.

So how is the minister to lead such a revolutionary institution? Eugene Peterson, a long-devoted minister and scholar, has provided a wealth of insight on the minister's role in developing disciples in Jesus' flock. His classic treatise on the ministerial profession is compiled in *The Contemplative Pastor*.[1] Peterson's first challenge to ministers is to be "apocalyptic" (others might say prophetic) in terms of being countercultural and offering alternative views to the mainstream values that dominate our increasingly secular society. One example Peterson uses is the concept of entering into the "unbusy" easy yoke of life with Christ. Peterson recognizes that this is a significant challenge, since contemporary culture is addicted to movement, routinely confusing it with progress, which too often causes us to run out of steam and collapse in the panic that the world is passing us by.

The pastor can choose to stand in opposition to such a life of disarray and instead assume a unhurried life of patience, confident that God is in control of the universe, which allows a demonstration of calm assurance and the ability to be present with others and with God while reflecting and embodying peace. Listening and being present takes time, or "unhurried leisure." For Peterson, using the adjective *busy* to describe a minister is parallel to describing a spouse as adulterous or a police officer as a thief. Hurry in the life of a minister of the gospel of Jesus should be considered "an outrageous scandal, a blasphemous affront."[2] In abiding in the easy yoke of Christ, there are no burdens of vanity camouflaged in the desire to be significant and effective. The long hours and the packed calendar tend to be strategies to hide from the fear of inconsequentiality. In the end, Peterson recognizes that such an unformed pastor living outside the ethos of the kingdom of God will let "people who do not understand the work of the pastor to write the agenda for my day's work because I am too slipshod to write it myself."[3] Such a minister is not leading a revolution of peace and grace, but is following in lockstep with the very cultural practices that require challenging, altering, and perhaps reversing. This is what Peterson sees as the apocalyptic challenge of the minister. As a leader, the pastor or priest is the one who "insists on kingdom realities against world appearances."[4]

The question Peterson asks is now the question pertinent to our charge as well: How is the minister to accomplish this? The last several centuries of theological education have suggested that the answer lies in ministers who manage the organization of the church. Peterson argues instead that the pastoral role is to attend to the "care of souls" and not devolve into the tasks of a religious salesperson or midlevel manager of religious organizations. Peterson defines the "care of souls" as a Spirit-directed, Scripture-guided, prayer-shaped calling of devotion to those with whom the minister finds himself or herself routinely in contact. These can be people inside the church but will often include those outside the church, in the neighborhoods, schools, governmental agencies, political organizations, and professional fields of law, medicine, business, and economics. The pastor's role is to follow God's initiative in the work God is already doing through tending, nourishing, and protecting those souls who fall under a pastor's span of care, whoever they may be and in whatever condition they are found. In reflecting on decades of pastoral life, Peterson muses, "Pastoral work, I learned later, is that aspect of Christian ministry that specializes in the ordinary. It is the nature of pastoral life to be attentive to, immersed in, and appreciative of the everyday texture of people's lives."[5]

I'm now old enough to remember a time when our lives weren't so busy and overscheduled. The evolution of our hectic existence manifests itself in several areas, but perhaps most obvious is the way in which we are raising our children. I pass by several parks and elementary schools on my daily commute, and I never see children playing baseball, basketball, or soccer without being in uniforms, with coaches, umpires, and parents on the sidelines. It wasn't always like this. When I was young, a group of six or eight of us lived fairly close to one another, and we played some sport or game nearly every day of the week. We couldn't imagine our parents taking off work to drive us to a friend's house. We rode our bikes everywhere. And as long as we were home in time for dinner, our parents never seemed to worry. There were no cell phones, the Sony Walkman was brand-new, and all we had for video games was something called Pong, which was saved for days when it rained.

Sure, we played Little League baseball and Pop Warner football too when it was in season. But they didn't consume every waking moment until long into high school. Here's my point and what I think Peterson is addressing: The church and our ministry leaders have unthinkingly acquiesced to the hectic pace set by our society. Therefore, too much of our church ministry is intentionally formal and organized so as to seem substantial and worthy enough to demand our time and attention. Rarely do we invite our neighbors into our homes to just "visit," as my grandparents used to say. We don't "hang out." Instead, we feel the need to impress, fixing a four-course meal, which requires cleaning the house, washing the dog, mowing the lawn, essentially putting our best foot forward to impress. This is not the ordinary, and it's not the real life we live either. Our youth and children's ministries do not have to rival the entertainment value of a Disney theme park to add value to our children's lives. The church has to be a place where we are able and willing to be who we are with those who are around us, modeling holistic authenticity, without all the formalities and facades. We need to relearn how to live and play together just for the sake of playing. We don't have to keep score; we can just enjoy being together. We don't need leagues, uniforms, umpires, trophies, and traveling buses. We just need to live together. It may be so "boring" we fall in love with the restful peace we find beside the still waters of the ordinary. To a society running 100 miles an hour with their hair on fire, can you imagine anything more refreshing?

To live a life celebrating the ordinary and finding authenticity in the mundane realities of our life, the professional minister cannot be alone in leading this quest. Ministers are but one part of the complete gifts given to the body of Christ. There are many talented and called leaders, spokespersons, and professionals who also must be equipped to follow their path toward discipleship to Christ. Therefore, it is the body of Christ, working in concert together with all the saints, wherein we are able to manifest clear and viable answers to the most pressing problems of our world today. Our world desperately seeks leaders, both lay and clergy, who are persons of influence who understand the nature and will of God. The many and various troubles within our families, marriages, social structures, and governments can be traced back to a bleak lack of knowledge of God and God's ways. The green pastures, calm waters, restoration, safety, security, and provision described in Psalm 23 are the life we long for and seek after. Jesus came to both correct and provide for that vision to become a reality, first in the church and then throughout the entire world. Professional ministers of the gospel lead that charge. There is no greater or more substantial opportunity. Therefore, great skill, devotion, discipline, and study are required for such a monumental and catalytic leadership position. But in no uncertain terms are ministers alone in their task. Nor is the organization of the church the only place where service to the kingdom of God can be contributed.

God's design for the church is very simple. Paul's metaphor of the human body allows us to imagine all our members or parts working together seamlessly to accomplish God's will. When this happens, people flourish. If it does not happen, then the whole earth groans. Pastors or priests have the opportunity to lead and guide the body of Christ as primary agents for meting out God's justice, healing, and love. Yet they do not do this by themselves. Instead, ministers must focus their energies on faithfully illuminating the minds and spirits of those in their care as to the nature of God— God's power, love, grace, and vision for all human life in the beauty of God's kingdom. When this is done well, as Jesus demonstrated and foretold, God will bring forth a bountiful harvest of workers of righteousness and justice into the fields that are ripe for harvest. These kinds of churches would necessarily overflow with disciples learning to walk with God in their world, choosing to seek and achieve for themselves and their neighbors, families, businesses, patients, clients, and customers the full blessings and effects of life with God on every human level. Paul illuminates this vision in his letter to the Ephesians. The ministers he describes (apostles, prophets, evangelists, pastors, and teachers) are not to *do* the work of the ministry as much as they are to *equip* the laity in their churches for living in and leading others to life in God's kingdom (Eph. 4:12). This is how the entire body of Christ is grown and developed.

Many ministers suffer from great guilt over the misguided assumption that their responsibility is to personally oversee every ministry activity in the church. Tragically, our congregations become paralyzed when ministers assume such tightfisted and overburdening strangleholds for leading every program, teaching every Bible study, and directing every event held when the church doors are open. Instead, ministers are to train and equip, for they hold the unique knowledge and skills for encouraging the engagement of the spiritual life, the life of the mind, and the practice of spiritual disciplines for character transformation in order for congregants from all walks of life to dwell on and experience the knowledge of God for themselves. When our ministers become trained and devoted to forming themselves and then others as disciples in God's kingdom, then our churches will resemble beachheads where God's presence and wisdom are enjoyed and shared, and where divine empowerment, responsibility, and blessing flow. There is one place and one place only that provides the incubator of loving sufficiency by which such a task can be accomplished. This is the church, the body of Christ, the hope of the world. And our ministers, both lay and clergy, must lead the way.

We can now summarize: Humans were created to live and work in the domains of the mind and spirit, which together work to transform our bodies through the application of spiritual disciplines from which we learn that, out of all the aspects of reality, God is primary and necessary. To miss this fact is to miss the most elemental building block of human existence. Sadly, such basic education is widely missing in our society today. To reiterate, perhaps more clearly, the principal responsibility of professional ministers is to faithfully and accurately represent to others the nature of God and God's ways so that people who are willing and able to listen (those with ears to hear and eyes to see [Mark 8:18 NIV]) can begin to think about and imagine who God is, who they are, how life is designed to be lived in community, and how the world is designed to work effectively in harmony with God's good will. This is the primary task of "caring for souls" for which the minister of the gospel is uniquely qualified.

If the ministers of God do not take the lead in caring for soul it will not occur. Again, no other leader or institution in our world today is establishing and protecting these priorities. As professional ministers appropriately pastor, teach, and encourage lay ministers in an efficient and effective manner, our societies as a whole will become increasingly overwhelmed by God's intention for holistic provision and blessing. Therefore, the role of the minister serving in the local congregation is to create a means of embodying and then manifesting God's goodwill in abundance by training individuals to be children of light who are ambassadors of faith, hope, truth, and love every arena of public life. When this happens, evil must flee as surely as darkness is extinguished, due simply to the presence of even the smallest light.

To seriously engage God's mission of revolutionizing our world and our lives now and into eternity, pastors or priests must reevaluate their current status and professional role. One of the factors that may need reconsideration is the amount of time and energy pastors should expend on the skills necessary to manage, develop, and advertise their congregation's specific brand of "goods and services" in order to compete in the spiritual marketplace of Sunday worship attendance. Again, we have stated that the purpose of the church is to make disciples, so pastors should be devoted to that primary task above all others. Religious consumerism and the pitfalls of this in our Western, individualist context make the difference between entertainment and worship difficult to distinguish. Yet the church, above all, must know and distinguish the differences.

The marginalization of the local congregation and the lack of professional respect for our ministers within contemporary society can be reversed. Such a task will require only well-trained pastors, priests, and ministry leaders in our local congregations and parishes who fully appreciate and then seriously undertake their calling to reassert their rightful and essential roles within our societies as beacons of this light. When this occurs, the body of Christ will model to the world the blessing God intended that God's people be.

 ## Questions for Exploration

1. What vision do you have for how the Kingdom of God might be manifested in your context?
2. Have you experienced or witnessed a situation where a ministry leader took too much responsibility for the success of their congregation? What was the result?
3. How can you best learn to experience the Psalm 23 kind of life?

 ## Notes

1. Eugene H. Peterson, *The Contemplative Pastor: Returning to the Art of Spiritual Direction* (Grand Rapids: Eerdmans, 1993).
2. Ibid., 17.
3. Ibid., 18.
4. Ibid., 41.
5. Ibid., 112.

Praxis Five: Leaders as Apprentices to Jesus

To accomplish the previous tasks of living a life in the Spirit and engaging a life of studious contemplation, embodying our faith, and leading churches into making other disciples who enter our world as ambassadors of Christ in every walk of life, today's ministers require a level of equipping, education, encouragement, and accountability as in no other period in recent history. Like other crucial professions, the ministry requires a long and dedicated course of study. But if living a spiritual life devoted to seeking the thoughts of God and God's ways is not connected to a life devoted to embodying the character of Christ, the professional minister faces a perilous future. For in the end, the hope of the gospel is to live, embody, and manifest the fruits of the Spirit of God's love in our individual lives right where we are. Therefore, the gospel of Christ is, in some very important ways, a revolution that begins and ends one heart at a time. And the minister's heart, mind, body, relationships, and soul must be the first to be affected by the gospel he or she professes.

There is an undeniable necessity for authority to speak about the things of God. Such credibility can certainly be bolstered by courses of study, well-written explanations, and eloquent sermons. However, in time, ministers living in a community, congregation, or parish will soon learn that lasting credibility is an outworking of authenticity. The minister who, year in and year out, is able to "walk the talk" earns a reputation that demonstrates the realities articulated by the written or spoken words he or she professes. I am not advocating perfection or even hoping to encourage ministers to elevate themselves on a pedestal of piety. Such would point away from the humility so desperately needed in ministerial vocation. Instead, I am advocating for a transparent and genuine demonstration of the fruit of God's effects in and through the minister's actions, attitudes, and achievements.

Therefore, spiritual formation, character development, and personal integrity are the final key components in the developing of an effective professional minister. The spirit, the mind, the heart, body, and personal relationships must work in concert to produce a complete, holistic minister of the gospel of Jesus. Ministers have the responsibility to become the type of individual worthy of the trust the public assigns them and their profession. They must have more than knowledge of the good, the right, and the ethical. They must become good, righteous, and ethical people. Such formation into Christlikeness will be as unique and creative as each minister God has called into service. Yet godliness is not an option for ministers of Christ; it is a certification of competency and evidence of the knowledge they profess. Of key importance to the pastoral role is the effective communication of what is good, what is true, and what is most loving so as to encourage congregants—according to their unique endeavors and callings at home, work, and play—to be agents of God's truth, goodness, and love within their spheres of influence. The minister is to influence the influential, to lead leaders, to guide guides, to shepherd shepherds, in every walk of life. Such a role is vital for the perpetuation of the purposes of God. This was Jesus' vision revealed in Matthew 28. As ministers do so, they mobilize the community of the church to stand as a city on a hill regarding all human endeavors, and they willfully invite others to participate in God's kingdom and its unique and peculiar ways.

Achieving the expertise and mastery of each of these key areas of ministerial life requires a rigorous schedule of training, study, and evaluation. Some may argue that Jesus' first disciples are an exception to this rule. I disagree. Jesus' first disciples devoted three years walking the hillsides of Israel, spending countless hours in conversation, service, reflection, study, debate, worship, and fellowship, all of which culminated in a level of character development and skills training that transformed ordinary Jewish men and women into outstanding, devoted, and effective ministers of God's message. Such devotions and ends were exactly what seminary training has sought to instill in past generations of disciples. It is disturbing, sometimes even tragic, to witness the current trajectory of theological education and the ways formal ministerial training are being marginalized in the local church. It is unclear how ministers can justify any claims of exemption from the accountability, responsibility, and integrity of character and expertise required of a profession devoted to the expansion of the gospel of Jesus.

When other professions are moving toward increasing training, advanced education, and ever higher ethical and moral standards in the accomplishment of their duties, to allow an increase in the level of isolation and autonomy inside many ministerial settings is a troubling—but perhaps a telling—indictment of current ministers' lack of self-awareness of their critical function in our world, and of lay leaders' failure to appreciate the purposes of professional ministry in general. Professionals can be held to account only by other professionals of equal training and expertise. The ministry is no different. Ministers are leaders and must follow in the footsteps of Christ, who was an expert in the issues of his day, demonstrated authority to speak on the matters he engaged, mentored other leaders in like manner, and was emulated by his followers, who witnessed the life he led, desired the peace, joy, and love he exuded, and therefore sparked a revolution that has changed the course of human history. Ministers of the gospel have no less a calling on their lives today.

Questions for Exploration

1. Think of a minister you know who is living the sort of authentic life in the Spirit of God you desire. What is most attractive about their life?
2. What is one thing you believe needs to be shaped or transformed in your life in order to better represent Christlikeness?
3. What is the one quality of Jesus that you admire most? How might you pursue instilling that quality in your own life?

PART

3

Forging Ahead

Let me try to offer something of a closing illustration to help us understand the need and opportunity that lie before ministers of the gospel in our contemporary era. On January 15, 2009, much of the world became aware of the inspiring six-minute voyage of US Airways flight 1549, scheduled to travel from New York's LaGuardia Airport to Seattle, Washington. Just a few minutes after takeoff, the Airbus A320 was struck by a flock of geese, causing it to lose power in both engines. Unable to make it back to the airport, the two pilots made the fateful decision to attempt a water landing. That epic landing in the Hudson River was played through the media over and over again, having been captured from several angles by onlookers onshore and through the windows of nearby office buildings. Rescuers were able to shuttle all 155 passengers and crew from the partially submerged airliner to the safety of the nearby Midtown Manhattan shoreline.

As a result of what New York governor David Paterson called the "miracle on the Hudson," the crew of Flight 1549 duly received national acclaim and numerous awards from organizations such as the Guild of Air Pilots and Navigators, the ceremonial keys to the city of New York, congressional honors in both the House and Senate, and a standing ovation at the start of the 2009 Super Bowl XLIII. Although the entire crew performed their duties with bravery and distinction, none was more deserving of acclaim than Captain Chesley B. "Sully" Sullenberger III, who was named one of *Time* magazine's 100 Most Influential People in 2009.

Perhaps a closer look at the facts behind the events of flight 1549 suggests that the notion of Captain Sully's water landing was the result of a "miracle" leaves far too much out of the equation. I certainly don't want to insinuate God was not involved in these events. I believe God was. But the story of God's work may be much more involved and grand than is hinted in the way the word *miracle* is used to refer only to the fate-filled six minutes of flight 1549.

For instance, Captain Sully had logged a total of 19,663 flight hours over nearly forty years of piloting experience prior to the accident. His first officer, Jeffrey B. Skiles collected 15,643 hours of flight time over his flying career. Added together, Sully's and Skiles's flight time equals more than four years of nonstop, 24/7 flight experience. It's difficult to determine how many actual miles that would be. One way to estimate the mileage would be to look at the longest nonstop commercial flight. The king of all nonstop flights, offered by Singapore Airlines from Newark, New Jersey, to Changi Airport in Singapore, takes nineteen hours and covers approximately 9,500 miles. An on-time arrival would require an average speed of 500 miles per hour. At that rate of speed, Sully and Skiles would have flown approximately 17,653,000 miles before climbing aboard flight 1549. That's equal to seventy-eight trips to the moon or nearly 709 times around the planet. All of those hours would naturally include untold numbers of differing flight conditions, weather patterns, pre- and post-flight regimens, flight plans, navigation scenarios, landing environments, equipment failures, technical malfunctions, and so on. The point is, these men were very, very experienced professionals.

Yet I don't believe the story of the success and heroism of flight 1549 begins with the endless hours of flight time. Instead, the stage for the drama on the Hudson River actually begins on April 3, 1967, on a small, undistinguished grass airfield that was owned and operated by a no-nonsense crop duster and part-time instructor near Sully's childhood home in Denison, Texas.

According to Sully's autobiography, he first realized his passion for flying on a spring afternoon when the then-sixteen-year-old high-schooler spent thirty minutes at $6 an hour in an Aeronca 7DC aircraft with L. T. Cook, a North Texas crop duster who managed the small airfield on his property.[1] After sixteen more lessons, Sully's first solo flight lasted only nine minutes. But that was more than enough to solidify his calling as a professional aviator.

Yet the most important lesson Mr. Cook provided his young mentee came a few months later and proved much more valuable than either could fully appreciate at the time. Sully recalls showing up one day at Mr. Cook's hangar and noticing at the end of the airfield the ominous sight of twisted wreckage of a crashed Piper Tri-Pacer. Mr. Cook conveyed the sad news that the pilot had misjudged the clearance necessary to avoid the power lines that stretched along a nearby highway, causing the plane to slam nose down into the dirt and killing the pilot instantly. As Sully took a closer look, the gruesome blood-splattered cockpit evidenced the great costs of mis-navigating the freedoms of flight. The young pilot absorbed the finality of the entire scene, emblazoning the undeniable realities of his chosen profession into his mind forever:

> I tried to visualize how it might have happened—his effort to avoid the power lines, his loss of speed, the awful impact. I forced myself to look in the cockpit, to study it. It would have been easier to look away, but I didn't. It was a pretty sobering moment for a sixteen year old, and it made quite an impression on me. I realized that flying a plane meant not making mistakes. . . . One simple mistake could mean death. I processed all this, but that sad scene didn't give me pause. I vowed to learn all there was to know to minimize the risks.[2]

And that is precisely what he did.

Sully went on to graduate near the top of his high school class of 350 and entered the Air Force Academy in 1969. Graduating in 1973, he received the Outstanding Cadet in Airmanship award presented to the top flier in each class.[3] The Air Force then enrolled him in a master's degree program in industrial psychology at Purdue University, where he "studied how machines and systems should be designed. How do engineers create cockpit configurations and instrument-panel layouts taking into account where pilots might place their hands or where eyes might focus, or what items might be a distraction? I believed learning these things could have applications for me down the road, and I was right."[4] From 1975 to 1980, he developed a distinguished military career, flying F-4 Phantoms; becoming a flight leader, training officer, mission commander, and aircraft accident investigation board member; and finally attaining the rank of captain before retiring from military service in 1980. As a commercial pilot with US Airways from 1980 until 2010, Sullenberger served the National Transportation Safety Board in several accident investigations and worked with the Air Line Pilots Association as the local safety chairman, instructor, and technical adviser. He also helped US Airways develop and implement training courses for airline crew members. He has also worked with NASA to investigate and prevent error-causing events in aviation. In 2007, he founded and became CEO of Safety Reliability Methods (SRM), a management, safety, performance, and reliability consulting firm. All of these accomplishments represent a lifetime of devotion to safety and excellence in air travel, all of which came to fruition on that fateful day, in front of the entire world, with the largest of stakes and the direst of consequences facing every decision. Sullenberger realizes:

> In many ways, all my mentors, heroes, and loved ones—those who taught me and encouraged me and saw the possibilities in me—were with me in the cockpit of Flight 1549. We had lost both engines. It was a dire situation, but there were lessons people had instilled in me that served me well. Mr. Cook's lessons were a part of what guided me on that five-minute flight. He was the consummate stick-and-rudder man, and that day over New York was certainly a stick-and-rudder day. I've done a lot of thinking since then about all the special people who mattered to me, about the hundreds of books on flying that

I've studied, about the tragedies I've witnessed again and again as a military pilot, about the adventures and setbacks in my airline career, about the romance of flying, and about the long-ago memories. I've come to realize that my journey to the Hudson River didn't begin at LaGuardia Airport. It began decades before, in my childhood home, on Mr. Cook's grass airfield, in the skies over North Texas, in the California home I now share with my wife, Lorrie, and our two daughters, and on all the jets I've flown toward the horizon. Flight 1549 wasn't just a five-minute journey. My entire life led me safely to that river.[5]

On a red-eye cross-country flight years ago, I ended up sitting next to an airline pilot who was deadheading from Boston back to San Francisco. He was tired from a long few days of flying but was very friendly and patient with a few questions I'd always wondered about commercial airplanes. At the end of the flight, we had what I thought was a fairly rough landing in the high winds around the San Francisco Bay. When the wheels slammed into the tarmac, I reached for the armrest a little too suddenly and grabbed his forearm instead. He patted my hand. I was obviously embarrassed, and we both chuckled. Then he leaned over and whispered something to me I'll never forget: "You know, flying is often endless hours of pure boredom mixed in with just a few moments of sheer terror."

Sullenberger's dedication, education, training, and expertise prove that preparing for those moments of sheer terror makes all the difference in the world. The decades of devotion to study, practice, investigation, instruction, mentoring, and advancement of both his own skills and those of his peers, and to the progression of his profession made Sully perfectly capable of navigating the potentially horrifying few moments of flight 1549 with calm focus, intentional and decisive action, and success. All the years and lessons that led up to January 15, 2009, are the components that together made the "miracle" we witnessed and celebrated. It wasn't one moment we witnessed. It was the culmination of a lifetime.

The same could be said for the actions of Moses in the face of Pharaoh's charging army at the shores of the Red Sea. Moses spent decades in the desert reforming his prideful arrogance and abuse of power learned in the Pharaonic court and became both trustworthy and practiced in how and when to wield God's power for good. Or we could consider the events that led up to David's triumphal moment in slaying Goliath in the amphitheater of battle before King Saul and all the armies of Israel. We often ignore the fact David brought time-tested and well-honed skills developed by years of slinging untold numbers of rocks in the solitude of the Judean countryside, then being tested under fire when lions and bears came in search of food from the flocks under his protection. Or perhaps we could even consider Peter's seemingly otherworldly ability to preach on that first day of Pentecost. We forget how well he was trained through watching and learning from innumerable conversations, teachings, and arguments Jesus engaged in as he taught his way throughout Galilee and Jerusalem. He observed and noted the tactics Jesus employed and didn't employ while facing the unceasing critique of the Pharisees and Sadducees. Such a course of study is precisely what Peter needed to see and hear in preparation for his own role as a teacher and preacher. These are only a few of the stories in the Scriptures that depict how God's grace and power work in and through those who are prepared, or are being prepared, to willfully obey God's leading and provision to accomplish God's will in whatever opportunities lie in store.

Besides learning from these characters noted in the Scriptures, we can learn from the examples of people like Captain Sully. His is a model that students, ministers, and educators today should seek to apply to our own unique professional callings within our churches and seminaries. Our society finds itself attempting to navigate the twists and turns of an increasingly secular world without tapping into the power required to do so. Too many lives and families find themselves adrift on a stormy sea of ambiguous virtues and values that misdirect our priorities regarding what is important, what is meaningful, what is essential, and what is worthy of giving our lives to. Yet life will not wait for us to make our decisions. Time continues to move forward, whether we are prepared for it or not. Our children grow, our parents age, our bodies fail, our livelihoods fluctuate, the financial markets rise and fall, economies shift, nations stand in opposition to one another, wars and rumors of wars forever lurk on the horizon. We must react; we must discern the best course of action for our lives in these shifting tides of global living, sometimes forced to decide between two less-than-ideal choices or sometimes coming to a point where we are unable to see a path forward at all. Where or to whom do we go for the wisdom, insight, counsel, training, and encouragement to navigate these tumultuous times?

Just as he did in the turbulent first century, Jesus stands before us, offering peace for our troubled souls; calling all who are weak, weary, burdened, afraid, and laden down by life's dilemmas; and leading us toward the abundance of rest (Matt 11:28). In him and him alone, we find sanctuary from all our fears and despair. The means for living in his ways, his truth, and his life are found exclusively in his church, his flock, and his family. The body of Christ is the haven of grace in a merciless world and an island of provision in our sea of scarcity and uncertainty. The steward, the servant of this sanctuary of blessing is the minister of the gospel. There is no one else who can oversee this responsibility. God has designed God's kingdom this way. When discipled leaders of Christ lead well, prepare well, train well, listen well, and learn well, people under their care and influence will live well. Captain Sullenberger's story perfectly illustrates that reality.

The books to follow in this *Exploring* series will engage some of the more practical means necessary to assist persons on the cusp of preparing for the ministry or, perhaps, to better inform local congregations and their leaders to pursue transformation of our individual and collective lives toward the righteousness available in the kingdom of God. The particular subjects will include overviews of the Bible and its interpretation, the important lessons of church history, and the role of theology in bringing clarity and the promotion of excellence in the soul-tending practices of the ministry.

Seminaries and schools of theology must focus on how Christian leaders and professionals can work together to manifest the kind of life Jesus describes in the gospels. Such a life must overwhelm our societies like a virus of goodness and love. What does such a life look like? How is peace or shalom to be the trademark of the people of God? *Shalom* can be understood as a state of holistic wellbeing. If this shalom type of life, lived in the light and sufficiency of God among God's people, is to become a reality, it will start as leaders and ministers of the gospel rightly take their responsibilities as servants and guides into that life. The following books will take us on the first steps in that very direction.

For those of us who wrote this series of books, our hope is to investigate the primary means of study and character formation necessary for mastering the divinities explored in each work in order for the professional minister to lead his or her congregation into God's kingdom as an all-encompassing, universal phenomenon of goodwill and human flourishing. Such a reality must include every aspect of human life—the economic, political, social, and religious arenas—as it becomes directed by the hand of a benevolent and omnipotent sovereign, Jesus the Christ. We now must focus our attention on what ideas must fill our minds, what drives must consume our hearts, what practices must form our bodies, what environments must represent our relationships, and what characteristics will describe our eternal souls. The next several authors will consider how our leaders are to be formed in these areas and then what shape our local congregations must pursue in order to facilitate God's mission in our world, now. For the kingdom of God is at hand. Peace and goodwill are available to our world and in our lives.

 ## Questions for Exploration

1. After considering the several praxes of Christian ministry discussed in the preceding chapters, what are your thoughts about the profession of ministry? Does it appeal to you? What is stirring in your heart and mind?

2. Which of the previous chapters most connected with your sense of what you would like to do with the gifts and skills God has given you?

3. What next steps are you considering to pursue your place in the mission God is working throughout history? What role do you want to play? What role has God asked you to play?

👓 Notes

1. Chesley Sullenberger and Jeffrey Zaslow, *Highest Duty: My Search for What Really Matters* (New York: William Morrow, 2009), Kindle edition.

2. Ibid.

3. Ray Rivera, "A Pilot Becomes a Hero Years in the Making," *New York Times*, January 16, 2009, http://www.nytimes.com/2009/01/17/nyregion/17pilot.html?pagewanted=1&_r=0&hp.

4. Purdue University, "Purdue Honors Hero Pilot, Alumnus Capt. Chesley 'Sully' Sullenberger," news release, September 2, 2010, https://www.purdue.edu/newsroom/events/2010/100902CordovaSullenberger.html.

5. Sullenberger and Zaslow, *Highest Duty*, Kindle Locations 252–61.